No Lex 12-12

```
J           16.95        139287
921.             PT.1188.89.01
DUNBAR, PAUL LAURENCE
PAUL LAURENCE DUNBAR
```

FLINT RIVER REGIONAL LIBRARY

PAUL LAURENCE DUNBAR

PAUL LAURENCE DUNBAR

Tony Gentry

Senior Consulting Editor
Nathan Irvin Huggins
Director
W.E.B. Du Bois Institute for Afro-American Research
Harvard University

CHELSEA HOUSE PUBLISHERS
New York   Philadelphia

Chelsea House Publishers

Editor-in-Chief   Nancy Toff
Executive Editor   Remmel T. Nunn
Managing Editor   Karyn Gullen Browne
Copy Chief   Juliann Barbato
Picture Editor   Adrian G. Allen
Art Director   Maria Epes
Manufacturing Manager   Gerald Levine

Black Americans of Achievement

Senior Editor   Richard Rennert

Staff for PAUL LAURENCE DUNBAR

Associate Editor   Perry King
Copy Editor   Terrance Dolan
Deputy Copy Chief   Ellen Scordato
Editorial Assistant   Susan DeRosa
Picture Researcher   Alan Gottlieb
Assistant Art Director   Laurie Jewell
Assistant Designer   Donna Sinisgalli
Design Assistant   Seth Wimpfheimer
Production Coordinator   Joseph Romano
Cover Illustration   Alan J. Nahigian

First Printing

1   3   5   7   9   8   6   4   2

Library of Congress Cataloging in Publication Data

Gentry, Tony.
   Paul Laurence Dunbar.

   (Black Americans of Achievement)
   Bibliography: p.
   Includes index.
   Summary: Examines the life of the poet and novelist who
battled racism and accepted the challenge of depicting the
black experience in America.
   1. Dunbar, Paul Laurence, 1872–1906—Biography—Juvenile literature.   2. Poets, American—19th century—
Biography—Juvenile literature. [1. Dunbar, Paul Laurence,
1872–1906. 2. Poets, American.
3. Afro-Americans—Biography] I. Title.   II. Series.
PS1557.G46   1988   811'.4 [B]   [92]   88-16140
ISBN 1-55546-583-8

CONTENTS

BLACK AMERICANS OF ACHIEVEMENT

MUHAMMAD ALI
heavyweight champion

RICHARD ALLEN
founder of the African Methodist Episcopal church

LOUIS ARMSTRONG
musician

JAMES BALDWIN
author

BENJAMIN BANNEKER
scientist and mathematician

MARY MCLEOD BETHUNE
educator

BLANCHE K. BRUCE
politician

RALPH BUNCHE
diplomat

GEORGE WASHINGTON CARVER
botanist

CHARLES WADDELL CHESTNUTT
author

PAUL CUFFE
abolitionist

FREDERICK DOUGLASS
abolitionist editor

CHARLES R. DREW
physician

W. E. B. DUBOIS
educator and author

PAUL LAURENCE DUNBAR
poet

DUKE ELLINGTON
bandleader and composer

RALPH ELLISON
author

ELLA FITZGERALD
singer

MARCUS GARVEY
black-nationalist leader

PRINCE HALL
social reformer

WILLIAM HASTIE
educator and politician

MATTHEW HENSON
explorer

CHESTER HIMES
author

BILLIE HOLIDAY
singer

JOHN HOPE
educator

LENA HORNE
entertainer

LANGSTON HUGHES
poet

JAMES WELDON JOHNSON
author

SCOTT JOPLIN
composer

MARTIN LUTHER KING, JR.
civil rights leader

JOE LOUIS
heavyweight champion

MALCOLM X
militant black leader

THURGOOD MARSHALL
Supreme Court justice

ELIJAH MUHAMMAD
religious leader

JESSE OWENS
champion athlete

GORDON PARKS
photographer

SIDNEY POITIER
actor

ADAM CLAYTON POWELL, JR.
political leader

A. PHILIP RANDOLPH
labor leader

PAUL ROBESON
singer and actor

JACKIE ROBINSON
baseball great

JOHN RUSSWURM
publisher

SOJOURNER TRUTH
antislavery activist

HARRIET TUBMAN
antislavery activist

NAT TURNER
slave revolt leader

DENMARK VESEY
slave revolt leader

MADAME C. J. WALKER
entrepreneur

BOOKER T. WASHINGTON
educator

WALTER WHITE
political activist

RICHARD WRIGHT
author

ON ACHIEVEMENT

Coretta Scott King

BEFORE YOU BEGIN this book, I hope you will ask yourself what the word *excellence* means to you. I think that it's a question we should all ask and keep asking as we grow older and change. Because the truest answer to it should never change. When you think of excellence, perhaps you think of success at work; or of becoming wealthy; or meeting the right person, getting married, and having a good family life.

Those important goals are worth striving for, but there is a better way to look at excellence. As Martin Luther King, Jr., said in one of his last sermons, "I want you to be first in love. I want you to be first in moral excellence. I want you to be first in generosity. If you want to be important, wonderful. If you want to be great, wonderful. But recognize that he who is greatest among you shall be your servant."

My husband, Martin Luther King, Jr., knew that the true meaning of achievement is service. When I met him, in 1952, he was already ordained as a Baptist preacher and was working toward a doctoral degree at Boston University. I was studying at the New England Conservatory and dreamed of accomplishments in music. We married a year later, and after I graduated the following year we moved to Montgomery, Alabama. We didn't know it then, but our notions of achievement were about to undergo a dramatic change.

You may have read or heard about what happened next. What began with the boycott of a local bus line grew into a national movement, and by the time he was assassinated in 1968 my husband had fashioned a black movement powerful enough to shatter forever the practice of racial segregation. What you may not have read about is where he got his method for resisting injustice without compromising his religious beliefs.

7

He adopted the strategy of nonviolence from a man of a different race, who lived in a distant country, and even practiced a different religion. The man was Mahatma Gandhi, the great leader of India, who devoted his life to serving humanity in the spirit of love and nonviolence. It was in these principles that Martin discovered his method for social reform. More than anything else, those two principles were the key to his achievements.

This book is about black Americans who served society through the excellence of their achievements. It forms a part of the rich history of black men and women in America—a history of stunning accomplishments in every field of human endeavor, from literature and art to science, industry, education, diplomacy, athletics, jurisprudence, even polar exploration.

Not all of the people in this history had the same ideals, but I think you will find something that all of them have in common. Like Martin Luther King, Jr., they all decided to become "drum majors" and serve humanity. In that principle—whether it was expressed in books, inventions, or song—they found something outside themselves to use as a goal and a guide. Something that showed them a way to serve others, instead of living only for themselves.

Reading the stories of these courageous men and women not only helps us discover the principles that we will use to guide our own lives but also teaches us about our black heritage and about America itself. It is crucial for us to know the heroes and heroines of our history and to realize that the price we paid in our struggle for equality in America was dear. But we must also understand that we have gotten as far as we have partly because America's democratic system and ideals made it possible.

We are still struggling with racism and prejudice. But the great men and women in this series are a tribute to the spirit of our democratic ideals and the system in which they have flourished. And that makes their stories special and worth knowing. ❧

PAUL LAURENCE DUNBAR

1

IMPATIENT FOR THE START

On A WARM June night in 1891, people from all over Dayton, Ohio, filed into the Grand Opera House and seated themselves in the first few rows. They had come from all parts of this growing city to applaud the graduation ceremonies of what the local newspapers were calling a "Banner Class." Making up the largest class ever to graduate from Dayton's lone high school, these were the only teenagers in a city with a population of nearly 80,000 who had elected to stay in school until their graduation that spring.

When the heavy curtains onstage finally parted, the audience saw just 43 students—the boys in dark suits, the girls in white dresses pinned with flowers. And among that group of Central High students, Paul Laurence Dunbar's was the only black face.

Missing from the audience were Dunbar's two half brothers, Rob and Buddy. Like most young men in the late 1800s, they could not see the use of getting a diploma, and so they had chosen not to attend their younger brother's graduation. They had dropped out

While Dunbar (top row, left) established himself as an outstanding student at Central High School in Dayton, Ohio, his classmates— including future aviator Orville Wright (top row, third from right)— were quick to discover that he was a gifted writer as well. Phrases from his poetry appear as chapter titles in this book.

11

of school years earlier and were making their way as laborers out of town.

However, the member of Dunbar's family who mattered the most to him—his mother, Matilda—was in the audience, beaming with joy at her youngest son. Nearly 19 years old, he had heeded her advice and completed his education. By earning his diploma, he had fulfilled one of her greatest dreams.

And yet Dunbar had accomplished more than that. His quick wit and friendly manner had helped to make him a favorite of his classmates. They had elected him editor of the school newspaper and president of the literary society. They called him "Deacon Dunbar" for the upright and dignified way he stood while shredding the argument of some debate opponent or reciting another of the poems he seemed to pen so easily.

Dunbar had worked hard at school, and he had worked hard after class to help his mother make ends meet. Now mother and son sat facing each other across the footlights, both proud of his accomplish-

Originally known as the Victory Theater Music Hall, the Grand Opera House in Dayton held a special place in Dunbar's life. It was the setting in 1891 for his high school graduation ceremonies and served one year later as the convention site for the Western Association of Writers, of which he became a member.

ments, and listened to the commencement speaker predict even greater things.

The speaker said that they were living in a time of terrific progress and opportunity. The nation had healed itself from the Civil War that had briefly torn it apart and was growing as never before. Soon the United States would take its rightful place as a leader in world affairs. The speaker charged the graduates to step eagerly into the next century, to create the machines and build the communities that would forever alter the face of the world they knew. "Life is all before you," he promised. "Your lives will be just what you choose to make them. Go forth."

To the graduates, these were not just empty words. Everywhere they looked a new world was emerging to take the place of the old. A few years earlier, Dunbar had hauled a ladder and a torch down the streets of his neighborhood, earning pocket money by lighting gas lamps at all of the corners; now, inside the opera house and along the street outside, electric lights burned, putting an end to that chore. Salesmen cruised the sidewalks hawking newfangled inventions that they called "typewriters," "telephones," and "bicycles"—all guaranteed to make life easier and more efficient. Doctors, the papers said, thought that organisms called "bacteria" might have something to do with diseases. Dunbar's friend William "Bud" Burns planned to look into that when he went to college to study medicine in the fall.

Another of Dunbar's close friends, Orville Wright, was absent from the stage. Bored with classes, he had quit school during the winter to build a homemade printing press in his backyard shed and put out a newspaper. Twelve years later, Orville and his older brother, Wilbur, would live up to the commencement speaker's words by building the first successful airplane. Yet they had already caught the spirit of the age.

As Dunbar prepared to enter the working world after graduating from high school, great technological changes were taking place throughout the country, including the use of electricity as a replacement for natural gas. Adapted from a photograph taken in the 1880s, this engraving shows a gaslit street in Ohio with lamps much like the ones that Dunbar lighted in his own neighborhood while he was growing up.

One of the few blacks to attend Central High with Dunbar, William "Bud" Burns graduated a year earlier than the poet. They remained lifelong friends.

Dunbar had that spirit, too. And he had a special contribution in mind. He wanted to capture what it was like to live in such an era, describing the feelings of people learning to live in cities, with machines, and with their memories of less hectic times. He wanted to write it all down and make it sing, so people could read his lines and begin to understand the emotions they could not put into words themselves.

College was out of the question for Dunbar. There was no way he could afford to go. But nothing could stop him from taking pen and paper and teaching himself to become a writer. Although Orville Wright could build a printing press, he came to Dunbar for the poems that were printed on it.

Dunbar had another goal in mind as well. All his life, his mother had taken in laundry from the city's hotels to keep her sons fed and housed. Her youngest smiled solemnly at her now, promising himself to find a good job so she could finally put her washboard down. Like the commencement speaker said, this was the land of opportunity. Dunbar felt certain that with his experience as editor of the school paper, he could sign on as a copyboy or clerk at one of Dayton's four daily newspapers. He would be a reporter in no time. With the money he earned, he might even be able to buy a house for his mother.

The commencement speaker sat down, the diplomas were handed out, and the 43 graduates of Central High stood to sing their class song. Dunbar had concentrated all of their hopes into the lyrics he had written for the tune:

> At last we move; how thrills the heart,
> So long impatient for the start!
> Now up o'er hill and down through dell,
> The echoes bring our song—farewell.

Dunbar went home, happily handed his diploma to his mother, and over the next few days began to understand that life after high school was not to be all he had hoped. His first choice for work was the *Dayton Herald*, a morning newspaper that had printed a few of his poems. But the editor told him plainly that the other reporters might get upset if he hired a black man. During the decades that followed the abolition of slavery in the United States, racial prejudice continued to be practiced throughout the nation, and blacks were virtually never offered positions of responsibility by whites.

Dunbar turned away, only to see an advertisement in another paper for a copyboy. It was just the job he wanted, but at the bottom of the page he read: "No Colored Boys Need Apply." The message was the same all over town, even when it was not said in so many words. By the time August came, he still did not have a job.

Dunbar had discovered the flip side of the commencement speaker's address. The factories and modern conveniences he had praised were drawing more and more people from the country to the city, where they had to scramble for jobs and houses. Black families from the South had been streaming north ever since the Civil War, and border towns like Dayton had come up with strict and tricky laws aimed at making it tough for blacks to find work or a place to live. People in some towns took even more drastic steps. In the year after Dunbar graduated from high school, 255 people around the country were lynched by vigilante mobs. Most of the victims were black.

Finally, Dunbar swallowed his pride and began to look for any work he could get. He signed on as an elevator operator at the new Callahan Bank Building downtown. The hours were long and the pay amounted to only four dollars a week, but in those days that was enough to get by. At last, he could tell his mother that she would not have to work anymore.

Going up and down in one place all day did not provide much of a challenge for Dunbar, but he was not ready to give up his dream of becoming a suc-

Dunbar had great expectations upon graduating from high school. Determined to become a successful writer, he was anxious to make his mark on the world by harnessing what he called "the spontaneous effusions of the poetic mind."

cessful writer just yet. He took a notebook and pencil to work every day, scribbling furiously in the minutes between answering calls to different floors. He studied his passengers, too, listening to the way that they talked, then trying to get their accents and dialects down on paper. He sent the stories and poems he came up with to newspapers and magazines. Most of these stories and poems came back, but one or two were published.

Then, just before Christmas in 1891, the Kellogg Newspaper Company in Chicago, Illinois, accepted one of Dunbar's short stories, a cowboy-and-Indian tale that he called "The Tenderfoot." Along with the letter of acceptance came a check for six dollars. It was the first time that Dunbar had ever been paid for his writing, and the check amounted to a week and a half's pay! He celebrated by spending some of his windfall on a big Christmas dinner for his family. And he began to write more seriously than ever.

Dunbar had been out of school for a year when one of his former teachers stepped into his elevator. The man, named Truesdale, looked at Dunbar's stack of books, then mentioned that the Western Association of Writers would be holding its annual convention in Dayton the next week. As a member of the welcoming committee, he thought it might be a splendid idea for Dunbar to come down and speak to the group. Truesdale said he remembered the poem that Dunbar had written for his high school graduation and wondered if he might come up with another one in honor of people who loved writing as much as he did.

Dunbar leapt at the chance. All weekend long, he drafted and redrafted the poem that his teacher had requested. Then, on the following Monday morning, he took off from work just long enough to run down to the Grand Opera House and recite his poem. Only some of the seats had been filled when

Dunbar graduated, but as he stepped inside on this day he saw that the hall was packed with journalists, authors, and poets from all of the surrounding states. These were his heroes, the men whose ranks he dreamed of joining some day.

Dunbar was introduced to the audience by historian John Clark Ridpath. If the young poet was nervous as he stepped onto the stage, he did not show it. Deacon Dunbar's straight-backed poise and steady

After being denied several positions in the field of journalism, Dunbar took a job as an elevator operator in the Callahan Bank Building in downtown Dayton.

Shortly after Oak and Ivy *was published, Dunbar reimbursed William Blocher and the United Brethren Publishing House (shown here) for the expenses incurred in printing his first volume of poems. Over the next 13 years, he had more than 20 books published.*

gaze quieted the crowd. Then, with simple dignity and the ease of a natural public speaker, he recited the 26 lines that told the writers of his admiration for their work. His poem ended with the words:

> To you who trace on history's page
> The footprints of each passing age . . .
> To you before whose well-wrought tale
> The cheek doth flush or brow grow pale;
> To you who bow the ready knee
> And worship cold philosophy—
> A welcome warm as Western wine
> And free as Western hearts, be thine.
> Do what the greatest joy insures,—
> The city has no will but yours.

The gathered writers applauded the poem, then clapped louder when told that Dunbar had written it. But the poet could not stay to shake hands. His job at the elevator beckoned.

The writers, however, were not yet through with Dunbar. The next morning, three members of the association tracked him down at the Callahan Bank Building. They wanted to know all about him: Who were his favorite authors? Did he plan to go to college? Did he have other poems to show them? But every time they asked Dunbar a question, the elevator bell would ring and he had to leave them standing in the lobby while he went up for a passenger. Dunbar felt ashamed of wasting their time.

Nevertheless, one of the three visitors, Dr. James Matthews, invited Dunbar back to the opera house that afternoon. During his lunch break, he stopped in and read another original poem to the group. They cheered this time and immediately voted to make him a member. With warm applause ringing in his ears, he again ran back to work.

A week later, Dunbar opened a newspaper and discovered that some of his poems—including "A Drowsy Day"—had been printed in a syndicated column, which meant that papers all over the country had printed it as well. The column had been written by Dr. Matthews, and every word praised Dunbar and his poems. The piece ended with the words, "Show me a white boy of nineteen who can excel or even equal lines like these!"

When Dunbar read that, he decided to try something he had been thinking about all year. He stopped in to visit Orville Wright and asked advice on how to go about publishing a book of poems. Orville could not provide much help. His newspaper enterprise had folded, and he and Wilbur were thinking about opening a bicycle shop to cash in on the new fad. But maybe, he suggested, the United Brethren Publishing House downtown could help.

Dunbar figured it was worth a shot. He went home, pulled out the big box of papers that his mother kept for him under the kitchen cupboard, and read all of the poems he had written. Then he pared away at the stack until there were just 56 poems left—the best of the lot. The next day, he put on his dark suit and carried his selections to the publisher.

William Blocher, the foreman of the print shop, grinned when Dunbar told him why he had come. This young black man just out of his teens wanted to publish a book of original poems? Didn't he know that books of poetry were hard to sell even when written by famous authors? Somebody needed to straighten this fellow out.

Blocher knew a quick way to do that. He told Dunbar that he would be happy to print the book if Dunbar would just hand over $125 to pay for the work. Dunbar kept his composure when he heard the figure, but he was shocked. That was more money than he earned in six months.

Thinking fast, Dunbar asked the foreman if he could get the books, sell them, and then pay his bill. Blocher grinned again. Who said anybody would be willing to buy the book anyway? No, that would not do.

While working long hours as an elevator operator, Dunbar used his spare time to write stories and poems. In mid-1892, he showed some of his verse to William Blocher of the United Brethren Publishing House, who agreed to publish the poetry in book form.

In the fall of 1892, Dunbar received a surprise in the mail: a letter filled with encouragement and praise from one of America's most popular poets, James Whitcomb Riley. Dunbar returned the favor years later by writing a poem about Riley that included the lines: "Now in our time, when poets rhyme/ For money, fun, or fashion,/ 'Tis good to hear one voice so clear/ That thrills with honest passion."

Stunned and disappointed, Dunbar turned to go. But the foreman reached for his arm. "Let me look at those poems," he said.

Blocher took Dunbar into his office, sat down, and began to leaf through the pages. He nodded his head from time to time at a particularly good line. Then he looked up and again reached out his hand. He told Dunbar that he would put up the money himself to get the book printed. All Dunbar had to do was make sure it sold and pay him back as soon as he could.

Dunbar could not believe his ears. A book of poems with his name on the cover was within his grasp. But if the book did not sell, how would he ever repay Blocher? Dunbar shook the foreman's hand and left the poems on his desk, but he walked out fearing he had made a drastic mistake. As the weeks went by and he heard nothing from the publisher, his fears continued to grow. Who was he to think that he could be called a poet?

Then, one day toward the end of November, a remarkable letter came in the mail. The letter, which praised the poems that Dr. Matthews had printed in his article, called Dunbar "my chirping friend," and added, "Already you have many friends and can have thousands more by being simply honest, unaffected, and just to yourself and the high source of your endowment. Very earnestly I wish you every good thing." The letter was signed by James Whitcomb Riley, one of the most renowned poets in the country.

Given such encouragement, Dunbar at last felt confident that he had done the right thing in agreeing to the publisher's terms. It was the biggest gamble he had ever taken. But it just might turn out to be worthwhile. ❦

2

THE UNSUNG HEROES

PAUL LAURENCE DUNBAR was born on June 27, 1872, in Dayton, Ohio. He was among the first generation of blacks born into freedom in the United States, and his parents, Joshua and Matilda Dunbar, swore never to let him forget that.

Paul's father had been a slave on a Kentucky farm in the years before the Civil War. He worked as a plasterer and was so good at his trade that his master hired him out to other farms in the area, promising that if he worked hard, he could eventually buy his freedom. Joshua Dunbar did not believe him. Even though slaves were not allowed to read or study arithmetic, Paul's father had learned to add and subtract from schoolbooks smuggled into his quarters by other slaves. He figured that by his master's calculations it would take two lifetimes to pay his way out of bondage. So he bided his time and kept at his work—until one evening, on the way home from a neighboring farm, he escaped across the fields and headed north.

Across the state line, in Ohio, Joshua Dunbar found white families who were willing to hide and

Both of Dunbar's parents grew up in Kentucky as slaves on farms much like the one shown here. When he was still a child, they told him many stories about slave life that he later incorporated into his poems.

23

feed him. With their help, he gradually made his way to Canada. These families were all part of the Underground Railroad, which helped many slaves escape to freedom in the North in the mid-1800s. Among the most celebrated members of this clandestine network was Harriet Tubman, a former slave who made 19 trips into the South to help guide slaves to a new life.

In Canada, Paul's father no longer had to fear that he would be captured and hauled back to Kentucky like an animal. Free at last, he took up plastering again. Yet he worried about his brothers and sisters in Kentucky, and when the Civil War broke

Dunbar's parents risked being hunted down like wild animals when they attempted to escape from slavery. Posting a public notice with an offer of a reward was one way in which a slaveowner could encourage the capture of a runaway slave.

$100 REWARD.

Ran away from my farm, near Buena Vista P. O., Prince George's County, Maryland, on the first day of April, 1855, my servant MATHEW TURNER.

He is about five feet six or eight inches high; weighs from one hundred and sixty to one hundred and eighty pounds; he is very black, and has a remarkably thick upper lip and neck; looks as if his eyes are half closed; walks slow, and talks and laughs loud.

I will give One Hundred Dollars reward to whoever will secure him in jail, so that I get him again, no matter where taken.

MARCUS DU VAL.

BUENA VISTA P. O., MD.,
MAY 10, 1855.

out in 1861, he made up his mind to help set them free as well.

Crossing back into the United States, Joshua Dunbar signed on with the 55th Regiment Massachusetts Volunteers, an all-black troop headed for fighting in the Deep South. The soldiers traveled by boat down the East Coast and saw action in the swampy battlefields near Jacksonville, Florida, and Charleston, South Carolina, where the first shots of the war had been fired at Fort Sumter. When the war ended—and slavery with it—Paul's father remembered the fine people of Ohio who had helped him take his first steps toward freedom. He moved to Dayton, hung up his blue uniform with the sergeant's stripes on the sleeves, and bought himself a new set of plastering tools. There in Dayton he met and married the jet-black woman with the almond-shaped eyes who would become Paul's mother.

Matilda Dunbar had been a slave herself, and she, too, had risked her life for freedom. Born in 1844 and sold away from her family while still a child, she worked as the house servant of a Kentucky farmer's wife. Although the woman kept schoolbooks out of Matilda's reach, she exposed her to music, fine food, and poetry.

Eventually, Matilda learned that her grandmother had been purchased and set free by an abolitionist from Ohio. Then she heard that her mother had also been freed. The two had made a home for themselves in Dayton. Because she was young and needed on the Kentucky farm, Matilda knew there was little chance that she would be freed as well.

It became even clearer to Matilda that she would have to remain on the farm after her master allowed her to marry another slave, a laborer on a nearby farm named Willis Murphy. Marriages between slaves were not legally sanctioned, and the newlyweds were not granted permission by their owners to live to-

A former slave turned abolitionist, Harriet Tubman helped several hundred slaves escape to freedom in the North during the mid-1800s.

During the Civil War, Dunbar's father joined the 55th Regiment Massachusetts Volunteers, an all-black outfit that fought against the Confederate army. In this engraving, the regiment is shown entering Charleston, South Carolina, on February 21, 1865.

gether, or even to see each other very often. The young bride soon began to plot her escape.

Still a teenager, Matilda Murphy set out for Ohio, but she did not get very far. It was not the slave catchers' hounds that caught up with her, however; it was freedom. On January 1, 1863, as she cowered in the hayloft of a Kentucky barn, she heard the slaves who were hiding her shout that President Abraham Lincoln had proclaimed their emancipation. As impossible as it seemed, they were all free at last.

Matilda Murphy turned on her heels and went straight back to her husband. Now they could live together, working for meager wages on the same farm where he had been a slave. While the Civil War raged in the East, she gave birth to two sons, Rob and Buddy.

Willis Murphy, worn out from years of backbreaking labor, died soon after the war was over. His young widow decided it was at last time to go see her mother and grandmother. She moved with her two sons to Dayton, began to take in laundry to pay her bills, and before long met Joshua Dunbar, a military veteran with fiery eyes and a courtly way of speaking. It did not matter to either of them that he was 20 years older than she or that she already had 2 children.

A year after they were married, their son Paul was born in a house at 311 Howard Street. By then, there were 2,000 blacks living in Dayton and competing for jobs. Because times were hard, Matilda and Joshua Dunbar worked long hours to make ends meet. When they came home, tempers often flared.

One night, when Paul was just one-and-a-half-years old, his father stormed out of the house for the

A year and a half after Dunbar was born, his father moved out of the house and went to live in the Old Soldiers' Home in Dayton.

last time. His mother turned from the door, wiped away her tears, and began to work harder than ever to keep her household together. Paul's parents were divorced two years later. Yet his father remained nearby, living in the Old Soldiers' Home.

While Paul was growing up, his mother continued to grow into the idea of freedom. She began to seek out all of the things that had been kept from her on the farm, the most important of them being an education. She picked up the alphabet from school-children and enrolled in night class for a few weeks until she learned to decipher sentences in books. Then she began to teach the alphabet to her youngest son while he was still in the cradle. She swore to herself that he would have all that she had been denied as a child. Like his mother, he had jet-black skin and almond-shaped eyes.

As Matilda educated Paul for the days ahead, Joshua Dunbar sought to have him remember the slavery of his ancestors. Paul's father taught him at an early age to stand tall, to walk and talk like a man. In a deep rolling voice, he drilled into Paul all of his anger at slavery and its brutality, told of his fear in escaping to Canada, and relived his army days in the swamps of the Deep South, where the alligators were as dangerous as the Rebel sharpshooters, and the malaria-breeding mosquitoes were more dangerous than either.

Paul's mother frowned at those tales. She was determined that Paul would not grow up scarred by slavery, even as recounted by someone else, so when she had him to herself she told him other kinds of stories. Hers were about good times: Christmas on the farm, sly tricks played on her masters, wading in the creek on a summer day. To emphasize the humor of these tales, she slipped easily into a down-home dialect, providing different voices for each of her

This certificate of membership in the African Methodist Episcopal Church was presented to Dunbar when he was 12 years old.

characters. Years later, the stories that Paul's parents told him would find their way into his poems; he would keep both his father's fury and his mother's humor intact.

Paul started at school about the same time that his half brothers stopped going. Rob and Buddy found jobs to help pay the bills, and Paul did what he could to help out after class was over. Despite everyone's efforts, the family always seemed to be moving from one house to another, where the rent was a little cheaper than before.

The family's moving meant that Paul had to switch schools, too. He spent first and second grades at one school, third grade at another, and then entered an

When Dunbar was a teenager, he was inspired by the English Romantic poets John Keats (above) and Percy Bysshe Shelley (on opposite page) to write about heroic subjects.

all-black school when he was in the fourth grade. Even though his family had to pull up their roots again the following year, he was relieved to learn that he could stay in the same school district.

Eventually, Paul's brothers married and started families of their own, which made things tougher than ever for his mother. For six days each week, she washed laundry for the city's hotels. To help her with her work, Paul gathered firewood and hauled water for her, emptied her tubs, and carried the clean sheets and towels back downtown. Sometimes, he hung out in front of the hotels, hoping to earn a penny or two for holding a horse while a wealthy guest stepped down from a carriage. On other occasions, he made extra change with his school pals by raking leaves and cutting grass at the fancy homes across town.

On Sundays, Matilda Dunbar made sure that Paul went to the African Methodist Episcopal Church. When he stood with the congregation to sing a hymn, he looked dignified and serious—thanks to the military bearing that had been ingrained in him by his father. Even though he was not tall, he carried himself with such poise, and he read and spoke so well, that his mother began to think that he might someday succeed as a minister. In the late 1800s, preaching was just about the only cultured profession that a black man might hope to have.

Paul started to write poetry in earnest at the age of 12. "I rhymed continually," he said later, "trying to put together words with a jingling sound." The idea that he might make his living as a writer never crossed his mother's mind. In fact, she made sure that he always did his schoolwork because she knew that a good preacher had to understand more than just the Bible. Paul went readily along to church, but he later admitted that it was partly because all of his friends were there.

At the age of 13, Paul stepped out of his all-black classroom into the only intermediate school in Dayton, where all of the other students were white. In the late 19th century, practically all of the few adolescents who could afford to remain in school were white. However, Paul was not bothered by the fact that none of his new classmates were black. He fully intended to make the most out of the opportunity to further his education.

Every Friday night, the teachers held an assembly to show off their brightest students, and Paul was soon invited to read the poems that he had been writing. Following one of these assemblies, a classmate named Orville Wright came up to Paul and congratulated him on the poem he had just read: a few lines about a black man who climbs a church steeple to put out a fire. After talking some more, Paul and Orville discovered that they lived along the same route to school, and they began to walk home together each day after class.

Before long, Paul and Orville became fast friends. They skipped rocks along the surface of the Miami River, fished from a bridge, and helped each other with schoolwork: Orville was a whiz at mathematics, while Paul was a natural in English and history. Both boys agreed that their favorite teacher was a man named Wilson, who taught them how to play a new game called football and introduced them to the great English poets. Paul's favorites were Percy Bysshe Shelley, John Keats, and Alfred Lord Tennyson, whose ringing lines echoed the heroism of their subjects. He went home every night and tried to imitate their verses about knights and maidens and mythical gods.

Paul sent his best efforts to the local newspapers, but his poems always came back. Then, at the end of school in his 16th year, the *Herald* printed a poem he had written in honor of his father, who had died

COMING

LOUISIANA COLORED MINSTRELS

UNDER THE MANAGEMENT OF
LEE CLARK

The GREATEST COLORED SHOW ON EARTH

50 CELEBRATED THEATRICAL CIRCUS AND OPERATIC STARS **50**

ALL FUN SHOW

Come and See--You Will Be Surprised

A RIOT OF FESTIVITIES SET IN A CANVAS OF GORGEOUS BEAUTY UNLIKE ANY OTHER PREVIOUS ATTEMPT IN MODERN TENT SHOWS

America's Greatest Singing and Dancing Chorus
WITH THE MOST WONDERFUL COSTUMES EVER SEEN IN THIS CITY

FUNNY COMEDIANS
ACROBATS
GRAND OPERA STARS
IMPERIAL Troupe of Tossing Turning Tumbling CLOWNS

THE BIGGEST BEVY OF SINGING AND DANCING GIRLS YOU HAVE EVER SEEN

In all the world no show like this. It is the only Big Show Coming This Season and you can't afford to miss it.

POPULAR PRICES

Everything Clean, Moral and Refined
FOLLOW THE CROWD TO THE BIG TENT

A popular form of entertainment in the late 19th century, black minstrel troupes like the one shown in this advertisement inspired Dunbar to form his own theatrical group. Minstrel shows were originally performed by whites attempting to parody the behavior of blacks.

4 years earlier. Paul had entitled the poem "Our Martyred Soldiers." It ended with the lines:

Sleep on, ye soldiers, men of God
A nation's tears bedew the sod;
'Tis but a short, short time til ye
Shall through the shining portals flee.

And when this memory lost shall be
We turn, Oh, Father, God, to Thee.
Oh, find in heaven some nobler thing
Than martyrs, of which men can sing.

Like the English masters, Paul wrote about heroes. However, his heroes were closer to home than the people whom the English poets had glorified. Paul had begun to see that all around him lived people who were as brave and resourceful as any of the heroes in books, and this was a lesson he never forgot. A major characteristic of his poetry throughout his literary career was his sharp focus on the nobility of everyday people.

Along with writing, Paul found yet another outlet for his talents, and he discovered a group of friends because of it. One day, when a traveling minstrel show came to Dayton, he went to one of its outdoor performances, and he decided on the spot to start up a theatrical troupe of his own. By the early 1890s, minstrel groups had been traveling all over the country for decades, performing humorous skits, singing songs, and telling jokes—all of which had their audiences laughing and crying at the same time.

Paul rounded up a classmate with a guitar, a couple more who could carry a tune, and others willing to dress up in costume to act in the plays he was writing. These plays were full of sword fights, cops and robbers, and cowboys, and because Paul knew that most of his audiences were to be found at church socials and reunions, he made sure that the bad guys always lost in the end. The troupe practiced at Paul's house, and he and his friends were soon performing almost every weekend. There was no money in it for them, however. They worked for free—and for fun.

It was not long before Paul's newfound friends asked him to write for the *High School Times*, which he was happy to do. He had been coming up with so many stories, poems, and dramatic sketches that he did not know what to do with them. When the Wright brothers began to print their first newspaper, the *West Side News*, on their homemade printing press in March 1889, they asked Paul to write articles for them, too.

The West Side News, *first published by Dunbar's classmate Orville Wright in March 1889, was a weekly newspaper that featured articles written by Dunbar.*

One day when he was with the Wrights, Paul wondered aloud whether a newspaper aimed at a black audience would sell. An answer came when Orville and Wilbur grinned at each other across the printing press. Before long, Paul found himself as the sole editor and contributor to another Wright brothers production, the *Dayton Tattler*.

The newspaper was only four pages long and came out once a week. Paul ran all over town drumming up subscribers and talking the few black businessmen he could find into buying advertisements. Then he ran home and wrote practically all of the articles that were needed to fill the paper. In addition to local news and editorials, he included original stories and poems. The first issue carried a western tale that he called "The Gambler's Wife," and in the second issue was a mystery romance entitled "His Bride of the Tomb."

Paul wrote, advertised, and distributed his paper while going to school, contributing to the *High School Times*, and performing with his acting troupe. At the same time, he continued to take on odd jobs to help out his mother and kept up his chores around the

Dunbar poses with fellow members of his high school literary club, the Philomathean Society. The club's Greek name signifies that its members are lovers of learning.

house. So it came as something of a relief to him when the *Dayton Tattler* published its eighth and final issue. Unable to find enough people willing to part with the $1.50 subscription price, he had told the Wright brothers that he was cutting his losses and discontinuing the paper. However, he continued to contribute to their newspaper, the *West Side News*, which was doing well.

Partly because of these activities, Paul was one of the most popular boys in his class by the time his senior year began. He was elected president of a literary club called the Philomathean Society and he led his fellow members in heated debates about the political issues of the day. Meanwhile, he and his fellow debaters poked fun at themselves in the school paper, of which he had been elected editor. One cartoon, printed in the *High School Times* just a week before they graduated, showed a serious-faced Paul and 12 other students all wildly swinging their arms in a fierce argument over the earthshaking question, "What is the butt end of a goat?"

Paul kept in touch with many of his friends in the year that followed their graduation from Central High School. Although some went on to college, most of them—including Orville—stayed in Dayton. They read Paul's poems in the local papers and congratulated him in the summer of 1892 on the nationally syndicated column that Dr. Matthews had written about him. They also congratulated him a short time later when they learned about the deal he had struck with William Blocher and the United Brethren Publishing House to issue a book of his poems.

Paul knew that if Blocher ever got around to printing up the little book of poems, he would have to depend on all those friends as never before. He needed them to help sell the book and make it a success. ❧

Dunbar at the age of 19, on the verge of seeing his first book in print.

3

A GLIMPSE OF GLORY

WILLIAM BLOCHER HAD promised Dunbar that his book of poems would be out in time for the 1892 Christmas shopping season. With that promise in mind, the young poet began to make a list of people who seemed to be interested in buying the book. He talked to lawyers in the elevator at the Callahan Bank Building, put up a flyer about the book in his church, and told his old classmates at Central High about the project. The *High School Times* responded in its December issue with this notice:

> Mr. Dunbar has been granted the unsolicited praise of some of the greatest writers in the land. His poems have appeared in some of the widest circulating magazines and publications in the West. He will publish a volume of his poems in a short time, and every high school student should procure a copy of the works of one, who two short years ago, was among us.

Dunbar also got a boost from the Western Association of Writers. Some of its members mentioned his upcoming book in their newspaper features, urging their readers to buy it.

With the groundwork laid to make a few sales, Dunbar paced the streets, waiting for the book to

As his first book of poems neared publication, Dunbar canvassed his hometown of Dayton for potential book buyers. Among the people whom he sought out were the passengers who rode in the elevator he operated at the Callahan Bank Building (center).

37

In December 1892, the High School Times, which Dunbar helped to edit while at Central High, advertised the publication of his forthcoming book, Oak and Ivy. *The school newspaper happened to be printed by the United Brethren Publishing House, the same company that was issuing the book.*

come out. His mother was at home alone when a messenger walked up to her door with the first box full of books. He left the carton in her hallway. Then, turning to go, he asked her, "Say, what is this Dunbar, anyway? A lawyer, a preacher, or what?"

Dunbar's mother, dazzled by the books at her feet and just beginning to realize what her son was accomplishing, answered, "Paul? Why, Paul is just an elevator boy—and a poet."

When the messenger left, Matilda Dunbar reached down and opened the box. Carefully, she removed a thin book with a simple green binding. The author's name was not on the book's cover. However, inside the book on the title page was her son's name and a picture of a tree at a bend in a road. Printed above the picture were the words *Oak and Ivy*. When she turned the page, she saw her son's dedication:

> To Her
> who has ever been
> my guide, teacher, and inspiration
> My Mother
> this little volume is
> affectionately inscribed.

Over the next few days, more cartons of books arrived and were stacked in the hallway. Blocher had printed 500 copies in all—some in green bindings, some in blue. He advised Dunbar to ask a dollar for each one. That would be a tough sell, Dunbar thought, but having gone this far, he agreed. When he handed one volume to a lawyer in the elevator, the lawyer frowned. "Mighty little book to sell for a dollar," he said.

Dunbar straightened his back even more than usual, looked the lawyer in the eye, and answered, "A book sells on its merits, sir, not on its size." Impressed, the lawyer handed over the money.

With that kind of conviction and the help of his friends, Dunbar sold 85 copies in 3 days. Within two weeks, he had enough money to reimburse the publisher; and by Christmas, the book had brought in enough extra cash to afford the Dunbars a big holiday dinner. Paul's gamble had paid off.

What did his supporters get for their dollar? They got 56 original poems, some of which would be quoted and memorized in classrooms across America well into the next century. The most famous of these was Dunbar's personal manifesto, "Ode to Ethiopia," in which he recalled his father's lessons about slavery and pledged allegiance to the honor of black Americans, especially in the lines:

> No other race, or white or black,
> When bound as thou wert, to the rack,
>   So seldom stooped to grieving;
> No other race, when free again,
> Forgot the past and proved them men
>   So noble in forgiving.
>
> Go on and up! Our souls and eyes
> Shall follow thy continuous rise;
>   Our ears shall list thy story
> From bards who from thy root shall spring,
> And proudly tune their lyres to sing
>   Of Ethiopia's glory.

Dunbar also remembered the lighter side of his education, adding poems in the voices used by his mother to tell her tales. The most successful of these was "The Ol' Tunes," the lament of a religious farmhand for the good old days in church. He exclaims in one of the stanzas in the poem:

> How I long ag'in to hear 'em
>   Pourin' forth from soul to soul,
> With the treble high an' meller,
>   An' the bass's mighty roll;
> But the times is very diff'rent,
>   An' the music heerd to-day
> Ain't the singin' o' the ol' tunes
>   In the ol'-fashioned way.

Here, in his first book, Dunbar had already struck a balance between a clear-eyed look at the way things are and a more forgiving glance at the way they had been. He would maintain this balance throughout his career and eventually find people willing to part with far more than a dollar to hear it. While people wanted to read about their own daily struggles in his serious poems, they also liked to relax now and then and recall simpler times. A volume of Dunbar's poetry helped them bridge the gap between their memories and the tasks before them. Whether writing in his own voice or in the dialect of a farmhand, he always aimed his work at any individual confused and pained by the quickly changing world. He sought to speak their feelings, to raise their hopes, and to help them through another day.

Although sales of *Oak and Ivy* dropped off fairly quickly once his friends and acquaintances had picked up their copies, Dunbar felt confident enough of the extra income to take out a mortgage on a new house for his mother. It was hardly a mansion, but it was

OAK AND IVY

BY
PAUL DUNBAR

DAYTON OHIO
PRESS OF UNITED BRETHREN PUBLISHING HOUSE
1893

The title page of Dunbar's first book of poems, Oak and Ivy.

large enough to have a room for boarders, a yard for chickens, and a garden. To help pay the mortgage, he began traveling out of town in the evening to read his poetry at church and club meetings.

Dunbar delivered his serious poems with a minister's measured cadence but slipped into character for the dialect poems, stamping his feet and grinning broadly as his booming, rolling voice pronounced the poems' songlike rhythms. The papers were quick to notice his talent for reading, with one reviewer writing, "For an hour he held his audience in delicious thrall, their delight being frequently evinced by loud and prolonged applause." Another reviewer added, "All agree he will make his mark on the literary world."

To cash in on Dunbar's growing popularity, the *Herald* hired him to write a few articles on local topics. This was the same paper that had first turned him down for work after graduation, but he did not hold a grudge. He remembered that the *Herald* had also been the first paper to publish one of his poems.

When the editor of the *Herald* asked Dunbar if he would like to go to Chicago, Illinois, to write an article about the World's Columbian Exposition—the first World's Fair ever held—he agreed on the spot. Both of his brothers were living in Chicago by then, so he knew that he would have a place to stay. If he could find steady work, he would be all set. Without any regrets, he gave up his job at the Callahan Bank Building and made his way north.

Dunbar found that there were jobs to be had in Chicago. However, none was better than the one he had back home. In a month's time, he worked as a waiter, a floor sweeper, and a washroom attendant. He held on to the last of these jobs because he had to put in only 5 hours a day to earn $10.50 a week. He sent some of his pay to his mother and spent most of the remaining money on exploring the city and the wonders of the exposition.

In the summer of 1893, Dunbar became an assistant to former slave Frederick Douglass. Working alongside the noted abolitionist editor and orator encouraged Dunbar to use his own writing to fight for equal rights for blacks.

Dunbar was amazed by the crowds of bustling workers, the black smoke of the factory district, and the towering white columns of the exposition halls. But more than that, he was amazed by the other young people he met. Every day, he ran into black men and women his age who were actors, opera singers, painters, or human rights activists.

Dunbar could not believe his ears one day when a young violinist to whom he was speaking admitted to being the grandson of Frederick Douglass, the celebrated orator and abolitionist. Douglass, who had recently stepped down from his post as foreign minister to the republic of Haiti, was in Chicago to oversee the Haitian exhibit at the World's Fair. The violinist led Dunbar directly to the great man's house.

Two days later, Matilda Dunbar received this awestruck letter in the mail:

> He said so much, Ma, that I must wait until I am with you before I tell you all. He had me read to him my "Ode to Ethiopia" and he himself read to us with much spirit "The Ol' Tunes," with which he seemed delighted. I gave him a book although he insisted on buying it. "Well," he said, "if you give me this I shall buy others." So I expect to sell him two or three anyhow. . . . I am in the very highest society Chicago affords.

Dunbar ended the letter by asking his mother to come up and see the World's Fair for herself. He told her not to worry about money because Douglass had hired

Held in Chicago, Illinois, in 1893, the World's Columbian Exposition celebrated the 400th anniversary of Christopher Columbus's discovery of the New World. The Haiti exhibit administered by Frederick Douglass was housed in the second building from the right.

him for an additional five dollars a week to assist him with his paperwork.

Throughout the summer of 1893, Dunbar worked side by side with Douglass as he met and entertained leaders from around the world. Nothing was lost on the young poet from Dayton. He saw that black individuals could carve a niche for themselves in the world and, with hard work and good luck, even change things for the better. Douglass, with his tireless campaign against slavery, had done as much as anyone toward that cause. Dunbar was inspired to see that the grizzled old fighter was not yet through with his struggle.

On August 25, 1893, Douglass spoke before 2,000 people at the World's Fair's Negro American Day festivities. White hecklers in the audience made racist remarks at the end of every sentence. Finally, Douglass stopped reading his prepared speech and looked down at his tormentors. Once again, the old lion roared.

"Men talk of the Negro problem," Douglass said. "There is no Negro problem. The problem is whether American people have loyalty enough, honor enough, patriotism enough, to live up to their own Constitution. . . . We Negroes love our country. We fought for it. We ask only that we be treated as well as those who fought against it."

By the time Douglass had finished, the hecklers were silent. Then he turned to the row of dignitaries on the podium and called for the young poet from Dayton: Paul Laurence Dunbar.

Perfectly in keeping with Douglass's stirring words, Dunbar recited a new poem, which he called "The Colored Soldiers." A portion of the poem declares:

Yes, the Blacks enjoy their freedom,
    And they won it dearly, too;
For the life blood of their thousands
    Did the southern fields bedew.

The most influential person in Dunbar's life was his mother, Matilda, who encouraged him to work hard and get a good education.

In the darkness of their bondage,
    In the depths of slavery's night,
Their muskets flashed the dawning,
    And they fought their way to light.

They were comrades then and brothers,
    Are they more or less to-day?
They were good to stop a bullet
    And to front the fearful fray.
They were citizens and soldiers,
    When rebellion raised its head;
And the traits that made them worthy,—
    Ah! those virtues are not dead.

As Dunbar spoke, his mother sat in the front row, beaming at her son as she had on his graduation day. She must have marveled at how far her son had come in three short years and wondered how far he still had to go.

For now, though, Dunbar had to pack up and go home. Although the exposition had provided work for thousands of people during its run, most of them— including Dunbar's brother Buddy, with a wife and two children to support—had to go out looking for a new job when it was over. The whole country seemed to be falling into an economic depression, and Dunbar had to admit that he was lucky to have his old elevator shift waiting for him in Dayton.

Before he left Chicago, Dunbar stopped in at Douglass's office one last time—to shake his mentor's hand and say good-bye. The old gentleman was waiting for him with a book of his speeches. On the inside cover he had written: "From Frederick Douglass to his dear young poet friend Paul Dunbar, one of the sweetest songsters his race has produced and a man of whom I hope great things."

Dayton looked small and dreary after all the flash and glory of Dunbar's experience in Chicago. He dragged himself back to work at the elevator, thinking all the while about his brief moment in the sun. But although everything seemed the same back home, he was determined not to let all he had seen fade into memory.

Restless now, Dunbar sent out more poems to potential publishers than ever before and began to accept speaking engagements in places as far away as Louisville, Kentucky, and Detroit, Michigan. Like his father and mother before him, he had caught a glimpse of a new sort of freedom. And like them, he began to plot a way to escape. ❦

4

PROVING THE WINGS

THE FIRST STEP in Dunbar's campaign to escape from Dayton in late 1893 took him straight to the Wright brothers. For their friend, Orville and Wilbur oiled up the old printing press one more time and produced a folder advertising Dunbar's services. The photograph on the cover of the advertisement showed the 21-year-old poet in his best suit, four-in-hand tie, and wing collar. Behind the glasses that he had recently started to wear, he looked scholarly and introspective. Beneath his photograph was printed:

Paul Laurence Dunbar
The Negro Poet Reader
140 West Zeigler St. Dayton, Ohio

Inside the folder, the Wright brothers crammed one of Dunbar's poems along with 17 testimonials to his talent. They made sure to include most of James Whitcomb Riley's encouraging letter.

Dunbar mailed the flyers all over Ohio and the surrounding states. He soon began to get more work, although he was never offered enough to give up his job at the elevator—except for one time, when he quit his position after a fast-talking promoter invited him on a concert tour. However, Dunbar had to go back to his job when the promoter left town without him.

At the age of 22, Dunbar began to correspond with fellow writer Alice Ruth Moore, initiating one of the most important relationships in his life.

49

By the time a local lawyer, Charles Wesley Dustin, asked Dunbar in 1894 if he would like to clerk for him—and, perhaps, begin to study law on the side—he was ready to think over the offer very carefully. After all, it was beginning to look more and more like he was wasting his time as an elevator operator. Finally, he said yes to the man.

Accepting this arrangement very nearly became a turning point in Dunbar's life: Studying law while holding down a full-time job did not leave him with much free time to write stories and poems. But he could not concentrate on his law studies. While poring over casebooks full of legal language or sitting in a stuffy courtroom listening to attorneys wrangle over minor points of law, he constantly found his thoughts drifting to other, far more interesting topics. He kept on reaching for a pencil and paper to jot down a rhyme or a clever turn of phrase.

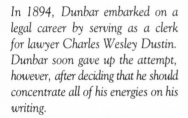

In 1894, Dunbar embarked on a legal career by serving as a clerk for lawyer Charles Wesley Dustin. Dunbar soon gave up the attempt, however, after deciding that he should concentrate all of his energies on his writing.

What was he to do? It was plain that a black man could never support himself as a writer. But could a writer be satisfied with making a living as a lawyer?

Dunbar argued the case over and over in his head while the attorneys argued in the courtroom. At last, he made a courageous decision. If Frederick Douglass and James Whitcomb Riley believed in his talent, wouldn't he be a fool to waste it?

Dustin was surprised when Dunbar told him he was going back to working on the elevator. The lawyer reminded Dunbar that he was passing up a great opportunity. But the young poet, determined to stick with his decision, just shrugged his shoulders and left.

Dunbar dusted off his flyers and began sending out his poems again. In December (which he now considered to be his lucky month) 1894, he sold three of them to *Century* magazine, one of the most respected literary journals in the country. Although he had been sending his poems to the magazine for nine years, these were the first ones that it had accepted.

Century published a poem called "The Dilettante: A Modern Type" right away. The first and last stanzas of the poem wryly expressed Dunbar's misgivings about his current prospects:

One of the keys to Dunbar's success as a poet was his ability to draw on his everyday experiences. After working as a clerk in a Dayton courthouse, he observed in "The Lawyers' Ways" that opposing lawyers will praise and smear a prisoner's character: "So, will some one please inform me, / An' this mystery unroll— / How an angel an' a devil/ Can persess the self-same soul?"

> He scribbles some in prose and verse,
>   And now and then he prints it;
> He paints a little,— gathers some
>   Of Nature's gold and mints it.
>
> • • •
>
> He looms above the sordid crowd—
>   At least through friendly lenses;
> While his mama looks pleased and proud
>   And kindly pays expenses.

Determined to do more than dabble at writing, Dunbar began to cast about in all directions for some way to make a living by his art. In addition to giving paid readings arranged by Charles Thatcher of Toledo, Ohio, and other supporters, he wrote letters to other poets, asking them for advice, and pored over newspapers from all over the country in search of new outlets for his work. In one of those papers, he found more than he had bargained for.

Printed in a southern journal was a poem written by a schoolteacher from New Orleans, Louisiana, named Alice Ruth Moore. Dunbar liked the poem. He also could not take his eyes off the photograph that was printed with it: The woman's softly rounded face held large, expressive eyes that seemed to brim with compassion.

Unable to decide whether to write Alice Moore a poem or a letter, Dunbar wrote both. In the letter—written on April 17, 1895—he did not dare mention how attractive she was. Instead, he addressed her as one serious poet to another, asking: What else had she published? Did she approve of dialect verse? What about political poems? The poem he included in the letter was about a sad fellow who might yet smile at the sight of a special girl.

It took Alice Moore a month and a half to write back. Dunbar tore open the envelope to read, "Your letter was handed to me at a singularly inopportune moment—the house was on fire. So I laid it down, not knowing what it was and I must confess not caring very much." But before long, she had picked up his note again. She added in her letter, "Your name is quite familiar to me from seeing your poems in different papers." She signed off with words that set his heart, like her house, on fire: "I shall be pleased to hear from you soon and often."

Dunbar was then editing the Indianapolis *World*, a black newspaper based in Indiana. His steadily growing reputation as a man of letters had helped him gain this temporary post. He immediately published two of Alice Moore's poems in the paper. When he begged her to send another photograph of herself, she did so.

In the midst of this romance by mail, the postman brought sad news to Dunbar: Frederick Douglass had died on February 20, 1895. Dunbar stayed up all night writing a poem in Douglass's honor, then read it at a memorial service in the spring. "Frederick Douglass" was one of his longest and most heartfelt poems, rising in strength—like one of Douglass's speeches—through 10 verses to proclaim:

We weep for him, but we have touched his hand,
    And felt the magic of his presence nigh,
The current that he sent throughout the land,
    The kindling spirit of his battle-cry.
O'er all that holds us we shall triumph yet,
And place our banner where his hopes were set!

Though Dunbar had lost one mentor, he was about to gain another. Returning to Dayton after his stint in Indianapolis, he discovered a letter waiting for him at home. As if its author had read his thoughts, the letter encouraged him not to give up hope in his literary talent. It said, "I believe you are especially endowed for this work and therefore would admonish you to continue as you have started, notwithstanding there is no popular clamor for, or perhaps much approval of what you have already done. . . ." The letter was signed by Dr. H. A. Tobey from Toledo and was accompanied by five dollars for copies of *Oak and Ivy*.

Although the doctor had never met Dunbar, he had read his poems, and he promised to help the young poet with his career. Dr. Tobey's letter was just the tonic that Dunbar needed. He wrote back that he had been doubting his prospects for a while, but now he wanted only "to be able to interpret my own people through song and story, and to prove to the many that after all we are more human than African. And to this end I have hoped year after year to be able to go to Washington, New York, Boston

Dr. H. A. Tobey helped Dunbar get his third volume of poetry published and made other arrangements that helped the young writer advance his career.

Dunbar dedicated Lyrics of Sunshine and Shadow *to Charlotte Reese Conover, one of his chief patrons, "with thanks for her long belief."*

and Philadelphia where I might see our northern Negro at his best . . . but it has been denied me."

Impressed by Dunbar's letter, Dr. Tobey invited him to give a reading in Toledo. When Dunbar stepped off the train, he heard the doctor exclaim, "Thank God he's black!" Dunbar blinked at the comment, but the doctor rushed to explain. "I meant thank God he's dark enough so that whatever genius he may have cannot be attributed to white blood," he said. This was a point well-taken in an age when many white people looked for any excuse to denigrate the achievements of blacks. Dunbar was proof in the flesh that skin color had nothing to do with intelligence or talent, and Dr. Tobey knew that this could make Dunbar into a symbolic figure in the struggle for equal rights.

While the doctor was assured by the color of Dunbar's skin, the poet must have been surprised at Dr. Tobey's appearance. The man who spoke so passionately about racial equality was white. And he was as generous as he was plain-spoken. Almost immediately, he offered Dunbar $500 to spend a year at prestigious Harvard College, the undergraduate school at Harvard University. That would have been a dream come true for Dunbar, but—kicking himself all the while—he had to turn it down. Five hundred dollars might pay for his tuition, but who would look after his mother and cover the payments on her house?

Then Dr. Tobey had a second idea: What if he and another of Dunbar's supporters teamed up to publish a new book of his poems? No strings attached, either. This time, every penny that the book earned would go to Dunbar.

It was an offer that Dunbar could not refuse. He selected 86 new poems for the book, adding 11 from *Oak and Ivy*. He made sure to include "Frederick Douglass" and a poem entitled "Alice." Intended entirely for a certain schoolteacher in New Orleans, the latter poem begins:

Know you, winds that blow your course
  Down the verdant valleys,
That somewhere you must, perforce,
  Kiss the brow of Alice?
When her gentle face you find,
Kiss it softly, naughty wind.

Of all the new poems in the collection, the most powerful proved to be "We Wear the Mask." In these lines, Dunbar captured the complex position that his fellow blacks, who had recently been freed from slavery, felt they had to maintain in order to survive in American society:

We wear the mask that grins and lies,
It hides our cheeks and shades our eyes,—
This debt we pay to human guile;
With torn and bleeding hearts we smile,
And mouth with myriad subtleties.

Why should the world be over-wise,
In counting all our tears and sighs?
Nay, let them only see us, while
  We wear the mask.

We smile, but, O great Christ, our cries
To Thee from tortured souls arise.
We sing, but oh the clay is vile
Beneath our feet, and long the mile;
But let the world dream otherwise,
  We wear the mask!

The poem speaks to blacks, yet Dunbar also aimed it at white readers. It is a challenge not to take black people for granted but to look into their eyes and read the pain caused by unfair judgment.

Dunbar called this new book *Majors and Minors*, once again dedicating the work to his mother. For the frontispiece of the book, which was published in January 1896, Dr. Tobey chose a photograph that was not Dunbar's favorite, although it cannily emphasized the poet's dark skin and Negro features. Then he sent copies of the book to critics all over the country, sat back, and waited for their response.

The most influential man of letters in America at the turn of the century, William Dean Howells called Dunbar "the only man of pure African blood and of American civilization to feel the Negro life aesthetically and express it lyrically."

At work in the elevator again, Dunbar may not have known the magnitude of his accomplishment, but he was soon to find out. On his 24th birthday, the nation's most popular journal, *Harper's Weekly*, carried a review by its most noted critic, the novelist William Dean Howells. Several of Dunbar's new poems were printed in the lengthy essay, which ended with these lines: "He is, so far as I know, the first man of his color to study his race objectively, to analyze it to himself, and then to represent it in art as he felt it and found it to be; to represent it humorously, yet tenderly, and above all so faithfully that we know the

portrait to be undeniably like. A race which has reached this effect in any of its members can no longer be held wholly uncivilized; and intellectually Dunbar makes a stronger claim for the Negro than any Negro has yet done."

Suddenly, people began stopping Dunbar on the street to shake his hand. Hundreds of letters poured in, asking for copies of his book and inviting him to give readings. Everyone whom he knew told him that he must go to New York City and meet with Howells in person.

Dunbar was overwhelmed by all of the attention. He may have thought that his book would be regarded as just another volume of poems. However, it was being read as a statement on behalf of his entire race. He had not set out to be anybody's champion, but on the strength of *Majors and Minors*, that was what he had become.

Dr. Tobey just smiled when he heard about all of the attention. Then he handed to Dunbar some money for a new suit and train-fare to New York City. With the doctor's support, the young writer had refused to give up on his dream of becoming a successful poet. And now, a year after first hearing from the doctor, Dunbar was on his way.

5

THE WORLD'S APPLAUSE

DUNBAR ARRIVED IN New York City in the middle of July 1896, and the steamy summer heat made the city seem even bigger, noisier, and dirtier than it actually was. He wrote to his mother that the city was "just like Chicago," but he admitted to himself it was a bit more intimidating than that. New York, the most heavily populated city in the country, was then home to approximately 3 million people.

Dr. Tobey had arranged for Dunbar to meet in New York with a well-known concert promoter, Major James Burton Pond, who had previously managed reading tours for Mark Twain and other celebrated authors. To determine whether the young poet from Dayton would be worth promoting, Major Pond invited him to read before an exclusive group of publishers. The reading went well. As Dr. Tobey expected, the major wrote to him that Dunbar had won over everybody with his stomping rhythm and imposing voice. His letter said that the white writers were "not in it" with Dunbar when it came to reading.

Major Pond found an apartment in the city for his newest client and immediately set out to win him a publishing contract. As he carried Dunbar's books

A view of New York in 1896, around the time of Dunbar's first trip to the city. During his visit, he gave highly praised poetry readings and signed on with a major publisher.

59

around to the commercial presses, the 24-year-old poet walked about the city, growing acquainted with a place where men rushed to cram onto a trolley even though another one was right behind; where millionaires in top hats and spats stepped over beggars in rags; and where ships from all over the world docked every day to unload immigrants intent on making a new home in America.

Within weeks, Major Pond found a publisher for Dunbar's work. Dodd, Mead & Company offered to put out a new volume of Dunbar's poetry, combining the best verse from his earlier books with any new poems he had written since then. The firm even paid him a $400 advance before any of the books came off the presses.

While Dunbar waited for his latest book to come out, Major Pond kept him busy, arranging for him to give readings around town. When Dunbar started into a dialect piece entitled "The Corn-Stalk Fiddle" at one of these readings, the orchestra behind him picked up the rhythm of his voice as he began to glide across the floor, clapping his hands to convey the spirit of a country barn dance. Among the lines that he called out were:

> So the night goes on and the dance is o'er,
> And the merry girls are homeward gone,
> But I see it all in my sleep once more,
> And I dream till the very break of dawn
> Of an impish dance on a red-hot griddle
> To the screech and scrape of a corn-stalk fiddle.

Before he was through reciting the poem, the whole room rocked with applause.

On another occasion, Dunbar was invited upstairs by his host to deliver a private recital to the ailing widow of Jefferson Davis. There Dunbar enjoyed the peculiar pleasure of entertaining the wife of the former president of the Confederate states.

Lecture tour manager Major James Pond handled the concert appearances of such popular figures as the poet and critic Matthew Arnold, the writer Sir Arthur Conan Doyle, and the politician Charles Sumner.

Dunbar's favorite reading, however, was given at the offices of *Century* magazine. This was the journal that had turned down his submissions for years, relenting only during the past year to publish three of his poems. After dinner, he read a poem entitled "When Malindy Sings." The group of journalists cheered. Then Dunbar turned slyly to the chief editor and said, "That's one you rejected."

The editor almost dropped his cigar but recovered to shout, "We'll take it yet!"

Dunbar waited for the laughter to die down, then finished with a grin. "I'm sorry, sir," he said, "it's been bought by another magazine."

Dunbar also found himself as a guest at fancy receptions and tea parties, where the lessons learned during his months at the side of Frederick Douglass came in handy. One woman who often saw him at these affairs remembered, "Dunbar was a man of charming personality with a bold, warm, buoyant humor of character which manifested itself delightfully to his friends. . . . When he found himself among eminent scholars or distinguished people in the highest social circles, he showed both by his manner and conversation that he felt he was just exactly where he was entitled to be. . . . His wit was decidedly pungent at times."

With the autumn of 1896 coming on, the invitation for which Dunbar had been waiting finally arrived. William Dean Howells, the man who had praised him so highly in *Harper's Weekly*, asked him to come visit. Dunbar took a train out to the beautiful suburb of Far Rockaway, knocked on Howells's door, and was surprised to be greeted with a bear hug by the distinguished old gentleman.

Howells had for years been the most respected man of letters in America. Yet he had not forgotten

Dunbar and an associate leaving Major Pond's home in 1896.

his own youth in Dayton, where he had worked with his father on local newspapers. He must have seen in Dunbar the same blend of talent and character that had helped himself come so far.

The two writers sat in Howells's parlor and talked all evening. Howells gave his guest a few lines of advice that any young writer might still take to heart today: "Write what you know. Write what you feel. Analyze detail. Build the picture. Make it real."

In December 1896, Dunbar's new volume of poetry, *Lyrics of Lowly Life*, came off the presses. Again, he dedicated the work to his mother. Howells compounded his earlier favor by adding a lengthy introduction to the book. This time, the old gentleman looked more closely at Dunbar's poems, deciding that he liked the dialect verse better than the serious pieces, about which he wrote:

> Some of these I thought very good, and even more than very good, but not distinctively his contribution to the body of American poetry. What I mean is that several people might have written them; but I do not know any one else at present who could quite have written the dialect pieces. These are divinations and reports of what passes in the hearts and minds of a lowly people whose poetry had hitherto been inarticulately expressed in music, but now finds, for the first time in our tongue, literary interpretation of a very artistic completeness.

Dunbar did not agree with Howells's assessment of his serious poems. Yet any quibble he had was quickly lost in the sudden popularity brought on by his book's publication. Because Dodd, Mead & Company was a major publishing house, the editors there could circulate Dunbar's books all over the country and even overseas. Thousands of copies were sold immediately, and *Lyrics of Lowly Life* continued to sell well for years afterward. At the age of 24, Dunbar had suddenly become an established author with a worldwide audience.

It was thrilling for Dunbar to stroll into bookstores and see the neat stacks of his books on the tables, and it was a pleasure to choose among the New York City newspapers that were clamoring all at once for articles written by him. He kept up with his newfound celebrity as well as he could, writing essays and stories, traveling as far as Washington, D.C., to give readings, and attending parties in his honor. He began to think that he might actually be able to earn a steady living from writing, making enough to support his mother and to begin thinking of marriage.

And when Dunbar thought of marriage, he always thought of Alice Moore. She had moved from New Orleans to Boston, Massachusetts, for more schooling; she was almost within reach. However, after two years of writing letters back and forth, she and Dunbar still had not met each other face to face.

Then an offer came that would move them farther apart than ever. Dunbar's book was selling well in England, so Major Pond suggested that the poet go there to further promote his work. To Dunbar, the chance to walk along London's streets—in the footsteps of his literary heroes—was an opportunity that he could not pass up. He begged Moore to come to New York City and visit him before his trip, but she lived with her parents, who were very strict and would not permit her to make the visit. The answer was always no.

A gala celebration was held for Dunbar in February 1897, on the night before he left for England. Beneath crystal chandeliers, top-hatted gentlemen jostled with ladies in expensive ball gowns for a chance to shake the poet's hand. Even Booker T. Washington, the noted black educator, came to see him off. Yet all of the hoopla paled when the guest of honor glimpsed across the dance floor the face of a woman he had seen only in photographs. Alice Moore had come.

Dunbar flew across the room to her and asked, "How did you get here?"

She laughed. "I just ran away!"

Again, the poet was caught up in a wave of hand-shakes and speeches, but before the night ended, he found a few moments to step outside with Moore. When his ship sailed in the morning, his ring was on her finger. They were engaged.

Dunbar stepped off the boat in England into a sea of publicity. Everyone wanted to speak to the man who so eloquently phrased the thoughts of black Americans. He wrote back home, "I am the most interviewed man in England."

Dunbar liked everything he saw there, from the Poet's Corner at Westminster Abbey to the neat gardens and polite manners of the English people. But most of all he appreciated being treated as an equal. No one looked down on him in England because of the color of his skin. During this burst of enthusiasm for the country, he wrote to both his mother and his fiancée, urging them to come and share his newfound paradise. However, there was no real chance of that happening. Even in England, he had to stay busy just to keep himself fed.

Major Pond had sent his daughter along to manage Dunbar's appearances overseas, and for a while she did her job. She arranged for him to read at private clubs and worked out a deal to have *Lyrics of Lowly Life* published in England by the same company that had printed the novels of Charles Dickens. But one day, without giving any warning, she took off for France, leaving Dunbar to fend for himself.

It was a tougher job than it seemed at first. Queen Victoria had just announced her Golden Jubilee celebration, so all eyes and ears were trained on her, with no time for the entertainments of an American poet. Not ready to come home just yet, Dunbar returned to his tiny garret apartment, where he made

While in England in 1897, Dunbar was befriended by American ambassador John Hay. A noted writer and historian as well as a highly respected diplomat, Hay was soon appointed secretary of state and served under presidents William McKinley and Theodore Roosevelt.

In mid-1897, Dunbar collaborated on a series of choral and orchestral pieces with the English-born composer Samuel Coleridge-Taylor, whose popular choral work Hiawatha's Wedding Feast was produced the following year.

the best of the situation. After all, for the first time in years he had free time on his hands without any obligations. It was the perfect chance to put Howells's advice to work and begin to write a novel. A few lines of verse from "The Garret," which was written at that time, show how much he enjoyed the opportunity to relax and just let the writing come:

> I write my rhymes and sing away,
> And dawn may come or dusk or day:
> Tho' fare be poor, my heart is gay,
>   And full of glee.
> Tho chimney-pots be all my views;
> 'Tis nearer for the winging Muse,
> So I am sure she'll not refuse
>   To visit me.

For Dunbar, slogging away at his novel was an enjoyable challenge. Yet his savings continued to drain away. Then, just as he was about to call it quits, John Hay, the American ambassador to England, gave him a boost. Hay, who also wrote dialect poems and admired Dunbar's work, introduced the young poet to the black composer Samuel Coleridge-Taylor, who wanted to set some of Dunbar's verse to music.

On June 5, 1897, the two men held a recital at a London music hall. The composer conducted an orchestra, a chorus sang Coleridge-Taylor's musical settings of Dunbar's poems, and the poet himself read aloud between songs. Dunbar had not been involved in a theatrical production since his high school days, when he had performed with his little minstrel troupe. The change of pace was just what he needed. Before the summer of 1897 was out, he had collaborated with Coleridge-Taylor on two more musical works, including *Dream Lovers*.

With autumn coming on, Dunbar realized that it was time to go home. His money was almost gone, and he had not brought any warm clothes to wear through a cold English winter. After all of the fanfare over his voyage to Europe, he now had to swallow his pride and write to Dr. Tobey for a ticket home. As he always would, the doctor came through.

Dunbar arrived in New York City tired and broke, but with a new manuscript under his arm and the dream of wedding Alice Moore in his heart. In New York City, he was still a celebrity. Editors jumped to be the first to get his impressions of England and requests came in from all over the country for him to give poetry readings. He accepted all of the offers he could, trying to pay his debts and finish his first novel at the same time.

One offer that Dunbar could not turn down was for a reading back home in Dayton. When he arrived there, the city turned out to give him a hero's welcome. Although it was unsettling to find himself the guest of honor at homes where, just a few years earlier, he had earned pennies cutting the grass, he was reminded by his old schoolmate Bud Burns, who had

In September 1897, Dunbar accepted a position as an assistant librarian at the Library of Congress in Washington, D.C. He had been recommended for the job by Colonel Robert Ingersoll, a prominent politician and orator.

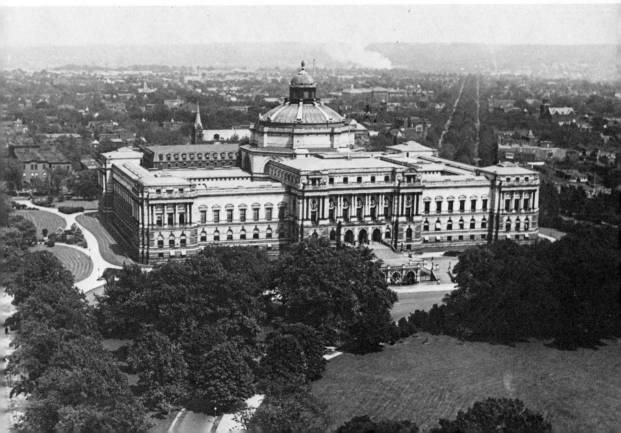

become a successful doctor, that he should enjoy every minute of it. Surely a poet could appreciate the irony of the situation.

Dunbar could not chuckle, however, over the irony that even with all his fame he could not make ends meet. He talked over finances with his mother, and she agreed that he should take the job he had recently been offered as an assistant librarian at the Library of Congress in Washington, D.C. He moved there in September 1897 and went to work stacking dusty volumes of scientific papers in the cavernous

Dunbar tips his hat as he leaves a Dayton church in November 1897. An advocate of worship that put less emphasis on rituals, he wrote in the poem "Religion," "Let Heav'n alone; humanity/ Needs more and Heaven less from thee."

stone building. For this, he earned $720 a year. When combined with his royalties, it was enough for him to afford a nice brick house near the library. With a steady job and a new home, he thought surely that Alice Moore's parents would consent to her marriage.

He was wrong. Perhaps Paul Laurence Dunbar was the most renowned black writer in America, but his celebrated status did not change the fact that he had never been to college. And wasn't he the son of a washerwoman? Alice Moore's parents, who were well-heeled members of the black middle class in New Orleans, told their daughter plainly that Dunbar was not good enough to marry her. The two lovers spent the winter apart: he at the library in Washington, D.C.; she teaching school in Brooklyn, New York.

Visiting her son in the nation's capital at Christmas, Dunbar's mother tried to help him think of a way to win over Alice Moore's folks. However, she could not come up with a solution, either. At last, her son decided not to bother trying.

On March 6, 1898, he stepped off a train in New York City, and in a private ceremony at which his mother was the only guest, he and Alice Moore were married. They spent their honeymoon night at a hotel in the city; then Dunbar and his mother took the train back to Washington, D.C. The new bride stayed behind in New York City to finish out her school year—and to face the consequences from her parents. ◆

6

'TWIXT A SONG
AND A SIGH

RETURNING TO WASHINGTON, D.C., after his marriage in March 1898, Dunbar mailed off his novel to Dodd, Mead & Company and touched up the last in a group of short stories that the company wanted to publish as a book. Then an old friend from the 1893 Chicago World's Columbian Exhibition showed up at his door, and again Dunbar found himself making music out of his poems.

The man at the door was Will Marion Cook, the son of a Howard University professor, who had trained at all of the best musical academies in America. Even with his impressive background as a musician, however, it was all but impossible for a black man such as Cook to find work with a classical orchestra. So he decided instead to focus his talents on the Broadway stage.

Cook wanted Dunbar to help him write a play about the origin of a current, nationwide dance craze called the cakewalk. Featuring struts and other improvised steps, it was danced in couples, often to the accompaniment of ragtime music. The term *cakewalk* was coined after it became a practice to award cakes as prizes to performers at dance contests.

Remembering the fun of making music in London, Dunbar agreed to help his friend. He showed up at Cook's basement apartment after work that very night. The composer later recalled, "Without a piano or anything but the kitchen table, we finished all the

Married to Alice Moore when he was 25, Dunbar wrote a number of tributes to his wife, including the poem "Twilight": " 'Twixt a smile and a tear,/ 'Twixt a song and a sigh,/ 'Twixt the day and the dark,/ When the Night draweth nigh./ Ah, sunshine may fade/ From the heavens above,/ No twilight have we/ To the day of our love."

71

songs, all the libretto and all but a few bars of the ensembles by four o'clock the next morning. By that time, Paul and I were happy, so happy that we were ready to cry 'Eureka!' only we couldn't make any noise at that hour so both of us sneaked off to bed, Paul to his house three blocks away and I to my room." The result of their collaboration was a musical play called *Clorindy: The Origin of the Cake Walk.*

Cook soon left for New York City, where he tried to stage the play, and Dunbar went there to get his bride. She had decided that she could not wait any longer to be with her husband, so she had quit her teaching job in March, shortly after their marriage. And to her surprise, her parents did not complain. Arguing with a lovestruck schoolgirl was one thing, but arguing with a married woman was something else. They did not exactly give their blessing, but they stood aside for the newlyweds.

That same month, Dunbar published a book of short stories entitled *Folks from Dixie.* The stories were like prose versions of his dialect poems. Most of them were about church revivals, hoedowns, and young love. He added one peculiar tale to the collection— about Southern servants who keep their old master happy by declining to tell him that there has been a Civil War—and he nodded in the direction of realism with a story about a strike involving black workers in the coal mines of Kentucky.

For most of these tales, Dunbar drew on the memories of his mother. Even though he had never traveled into Dixie himself, he still managed to impress readers with his understanding of the South. One reviewer wrote that the book was "notable as the first expression in national prose fiction of the inner life of the American Negro."

Proud of her literary husband, the new Mrs. Dunbar, being a writer herself—she had recently published *Violets and Other Tales*—hoped to share in the spotlight someday. She had already begun writing *Goodness of St. Rocque*, a collection of short stories about life in New Orleans, which was printed by her husband's publisher the following year. Their marriage, it seemed, would bring them a lifetime of happiness and success.

But Dunbar was keeping a secret from Alice, and she soon found out what it was. One night, she awoke to find her husband wracked with coughs, barely able to breathe. Terrified, she wrapped him in a blanket and waited for the attack to subside. When she asked him how long he had been having this trouble, he answered weakly that it had been going on for a while.

From that moment on, Alice stood vigil over her husband's health. She saw how he worked himself to the bone by giving readings, writing until all hours of the night, and putting in long days at the library. She blamed his illness on this last activity. The aisles, lined with dark bookshelves, were dusty and stiflingly hot. America's favorite young poet had no business hauling scientific tomes back and forth all day, Alice felt. The work was wrecking his lungs. Convinced that they could get by on royalties from their books, she launched a steady campaign to get him to quit his job.

Meanwhile, Cook had completed rehearsals for *Clorindy*. The newlyweds took a train to New York City for the show's gala opening at the Casino Roof Garden, and if they were not surprised at the play's blend of high energy and excitement, everybody else in the city seemed to be. Stuffy white critics were treated to high-stepping black actors dancing and singing at the same time. It is easy to imagine a poem such as Dunbar's "Jump Back Honey," which includes the following lines, made into the rousing syncopated dance number it had become:

Dunbar teamed up with musician Will Marion Cook to write several theatrical pieces. Their first effort, Clorindy, was their most successful one as well.

Put my ahm aroun' huh wais'
  Jump back, honey, jump back.
Raised huh lips an' took a tase,
  Jump back, honey, jump back.
Love me, honey, love me true?
  Love me well ez I love you?
An' she answe'd, "'Cose I do"—
  Jump back, honey, jump back.

A huge rooftop theater in New York City, the Casino Roof Garden was the site of the premiere engagement of Clorindy *in 1898. The midtown theater is shown here as it looked in the mid-1890s.*

The Dunbars spent most of their vacation in the midtown neighborhood known as the Tenderloin, where most of the city's black artists and musicians lived and worked. (The uptown district known as Harlem, which became the nation's largest black residential area 20 years later, was then a community of wealthy and working-class whites.) As before, Dunbar found himself marveling at the urban haven

that his fellow blacks seemed to be carving for themselves in New York City.

Meanwhile, those people marveled at Dunbar. James Weldon Johnson, an aspiring poet who had met Dunbar at the World's Columbian Exposition and was about to move to New York City, said of his much-admired friend: "When he walked into the hall all those who knew him rushed to welcome him, and among those who did not know him personally there were awed whispers. But it did not appear that celebrity had puffed him up." Nevertheless, the popular poet managed to convey an air of distinction. According to Johnson, "He had an innate courtliness of manner, his speech was unaffectedly polished and brilliant, and he carried himself with the dignity of humility which never fails to produce a sense of the presence of greatness."

Dunbar's good humor was helped along by the reception of *Clorindy*, which played nightly at the Casino all summer long and was a huge success. By the time the show went on the road to most of the big cities along the East Coast, he was back home in Washington, D.C., his coughing fits having grown worse. He wrote to a friend that he was unhealthy and unhappy at his job, adding, "I am in love with literature and wish I could give my whole time to reading and writing, but alas! one must eat, and so I plod along, making the thing that is really first in my heart, secondary in my life."

When October 1898 came, Dunbar had something new to be unhappy about: the first negative reviews of his writing. The subject of these reviews was *The Uncalled*. His first novel, it tells the story of a young man who rebels against his adoptive parents' ambition for him to become a minister.

In the novel, Dunbar wanted to show that there was more to being religious than just going to church. Consequently, when the main character is accused of having forsaken his religion, he replies, "I've just come to know what religion is. It's to be bigger and broader and kinder, and to live and to love and be happy, so that people around you will be happy." Dunbar might have used words like these in answer to his mother years earlier, when she had dreamed of him becoming a preacher.

The book set off a wild debate around the country, but not on religious grounds. Dunbar had chosen to make the main character a white man, and some critics would not stand for that. "Why doesn't he stick to writing about Negroes?" they wrote.

Other critics defended the book, asking why it was fine for white writers to portray blacks but wrong for a black writer to focus on whites. Remembering his old friendships with the Wright brothers and other white families back in Dayton, Dunbar figured that he understood whites as well as anybody. He also sensed that the critics who had attacked him wanted to pigeonhole him as a black writer unqualified to address any other topic. Wasn't that really what they meant when they praised his dialect poems and neglected the others? Even his mentor William Dean Howells had treated his work that way.

Dunbar could see that it was time to take a sharp look at his career and head in a new direction. He knew that the mistreatment he was receiving amounted to nothing when compared with the difficulties of other blacks, and he decided that it was time to speak out more strongly against the rising tide of racism in the country. Soon, the newspapers that were always clamoring for Dunbar to write an optimistic article for them began to get scathing critiques of racial injustice instead.

Hearing that black soldiers who had just fought in the Spanish-American War were being denied the right to vote in some states, Dunbar attempted to point out the hypocrisy of the American government.

An author, educator, songwriter, and diplomat, Dunbar's multitalented friend James Weldon Johnson became the chief executive of the National Association for the Advancement of Colored People (NAACP) in the 1920s.

He wrote that with this denial, the government was in effect saying to blacks: "You may fight for us but you may not vote for us. You may prove a strong bulwark when the bullets are flying but you must stand from the line when the ballots are in the air. You may be heroes in war but you must be cravens in peace."

In another article, which he wrote after a race riot in Wilmington, North Carolina, Dunbar recalled the speech that Frederick Douglass had given at the Chicago World's Columbian Exhibition: "After all, the question is not the Negro's fitness to rule or vote, but of the white's right to murder him for the sake of instruction. . . . It will take more than lynchings to make the Negro believe he is not an American citizen when the Constitution says he is." Until the end of his life, Dunbar kept up his battle in the press, offering cool reason to fight against the fires of racism.

To this day, some people have chosen to regard Dunbar only as a dialect poet. They say that his writings made blacks look like happy-go-lucky farm folks without a care in the world. But his dialect poems achieved more than that. In those poems, he looked at a wide variety of individuals, spoke in their voices, and showed that there is humor and spirit even in the most difficult lives.

In his more serious poems, Dunbar went further, baring his own soul in eloquent lines that proved even to the most ardent racist that a black man could express deep thoughts and feelings as movingly as anyone else. His stories, which ranged all over America, painted whites and blacks living together and apart, and the main achievement in these stories lay in his fairness. He exposed the flawed thinking of racists without making them into monsters, and he admitted that blacks sometimes fight among themselves.

The dealings of black and white people in America are often complex and difficult to see clearly, but Dunbar knew that he was in a unique position to contribute to an understanding between the races. Consequently, the old fire of his father and of Frederick Douglass flamed again in the articles and essays that he wrote after the publication of *The Uncalled*. The poet used these works to look with a sharp eye at day-to-day events and dared his readers to ignore racial injustice.

There were many sides to Paul Laurence Dunbar, as there are to any man or woman, and the reader of just his poems, or just his stories, misses a part of him. In his articles, most of which were printed in newspapers that are long gone today, he proved him-

THE NEW YORK TIMES, FRIDAY, JULY 10, 1903

10,000 EXCURSIONISTS SUNG TO BY GRUBER

He Was in Charge of Riverside Republican Club's Outing.

Three Steamer Loads of Merrymakers Forced to Listen to an Original Lullaby—Picnic a "Howling" Success.

Col. Abraham Gruber, who prefers to be called "Col. Abe," and is most flattered when addressed by his constituents as "Abe," was in charge of the ninth annual excursion of the Riverside Republican Club of the Twenty-first Assembly District yesterday, and saw to it personally that the 10,000 women and children and incidentally the men all got aboard the three steamers chartered for the day from the Iron Steamboat Line. He was aided by lieutenants of the regular Republican organization and a detail of policemen from the West One Hundredth Street Police Station.

There were three steamers, the Cepheus, the Taurus, and the Sirius. As the people gathered at the appointed hour, 9 o'clock, at the West Ninety-sixth Street dock, in what looked like vast multitudes, it seemed that an order would have to be given to charter more boats. It may have been that some could not stand the heat and returned to their homes, but it is probable that the order was not sent for more floating accommodations because Col. Abe burst forth into song. He had written the verses, and as he could find no one to fit music to them, he did the best he could with the result that the three boats, though packed to their utmost capacity, and, according to his Democratic enemies, beyond the limit of the law, barely held the crowd.

There was a band on each boat, and for a while they did their best to drown Col. Abe when he would bring to the waiting thousands a breeze as he exercised his vocal cords. The handling of the women pushing baby carriages, the small boys who dubbed the latter "automobubilies " the little girls who felt it necessary to take along with them their precious dolls, and the old men and women, was admirable. There was a Corporal's guard of young men, loyal to the chief, to see to it that everybody had a good time, even if they had to dance with a dozen girls in every waltz and two-step on the way, to Laurel Grove on the Sound.

The 10,000 excursionists crowded or the three boats were under way shortly before 10 o'clock. "Col. Abe" was on the last boat. A committee saved him from jumping overboard to rescue the few who were too late and in danger of falling into the river in the hope that the boats might stop to take them aboard.

"Col. Abe" had his chance when the excursion was in midstream, well under way, and the boats about a mile apart. The other boats in the river stopped their three-blast saluting because their skippers real-

BURGLARIES IN DAYLIGHT.

Two Families Who Came Here from Chicago to Escape Burglars Lose Their Valuables.

Two burglaries, in which the residences of Louis Enright, a civil engineer, at 799 East One Hundred and Eighty-third Street, and that of Charles D'Almaine, the first violinist at the Broadway Theatre, at 1,371 Hughes Avenue, were looted of silverware and jewelry to the total amount of about $3,000, have been reported to the police of the Tremont Station.

Both burglaries were committed in broad daylight in full view of persons in the street. A peculiar phase of the case is that both the Enright and D'Almaine families came here recently from Chicago, the Enrights taking up their residence here for the express purpose of getting away from burglars in Chicago, which were looting houses by the wholesale when the family left that city.

Mr. and Mrs. Enright and son left the house at 7 o'clock Wednesday morning for a trip to the country. When they returned early in the evening the family noticed that the front door of their house was open. An investigation showed that burglars had forced the cellar door, which is plainly visible from the street. The bureau drawers in every room had been taken out and their contents strewn on the floor. The burglars had discriminated between the solid and plated silverware, taking all of the former and leaving the latter. Several hundred dollars' worth of jewelry had been stolen.

The D'Almaine residence was burglarized last Thursday during the thunderstorm that took place in the afternoon. Mrs. D'Almaine went to a neighbor's house during the storm, returning when the rain had ceased. Her house had been entered also by the cellar door.

The burglars again showed a similar preference for solid silverware over the plated, as in the other burglary, and the police think the same men were implicated in both robberies.

SAVED PIECES OF TORN CHECK.

Then Samuel Epstein Cashed Them and He Is Arrested Charged with Grand Larceny.

Samuel Epstein, thirty-two years old, of 2,337 Third Avenue, was arrested last night by Detectives Shafer and Lister and was locked up in the East One Hundred and Twenty-sixth Street Police Station, charged with grand larceny. Several days ago City Marshal Matthew Mulvihill had occasion to pay him a bill of $75. As he did not have the ready money at hand he offered Epstein a check.

Epstein did not want the check and said so, and after tearing it in two Mulvihill offered him $25 in cash and a check for $50. This was satisfactory, but when Mulvihill was making out the check Epstein picked up the two pieces of the $75 check from the floor, and on the following day, after pasting them together, cashed it.

Then the Marshal sent for the detectives, and had him arrested. When he was taken from his home his wife Sarah became hysterical and then fainted and had to be

THE FOURTH OF JULY AND RACE OUTRAGES

Paul Laurence Dunbar's Bitter Satire on Independence Day.

Negro Poet Speaks for His Race in Burning Words, and Says God's Justice is Made a Jest.

Special to The New York Times.

CHICAGO, July 9.—The recent race riots at Evansville, following so closely on similar occurrences at Belleville and Wilmington, have caused Paul Laurence Dunbar, the negro author, to write the following note of protest:

"Belleville, Wilmington, Evansville, the Fourth of July, and Kishineff, a curious combination and yet one replete with a ghastly humor. Sitting with closed lips over our own bloody deeds we accomplish the fine irony of a protest to Russia. Contemplating with placid eyes the destruction of all the Declaration of Independence and the Constitution stood for, we celebrate the thing which our own action proclaims we do not believe in.

"But it is over and done. The Fourth is come and gone. The din has ceased and the smoke has cleared away. Nothing remains but the litter of all and a few reflections. The skyrocket has ascended, the firecrackers have burst, the roman candles have sputtered, the 'nigger chasers'—a pertinent American name—have run their course, and we have celebrated the Nation's birthday. Yes, and we black folks have celebrated.

"Dearborn Street and Armour Avenue have been all life and light. Not even the Jew and the Chinaman have been able to outdo us in the display of loyalty. And we have done it all because we have not stopped to think just how little it means to us.

"The papers are full of the reports of peonage in Alabama. A new and more dastardly slavery there has arisen to replace the old. For the sake of re-enslaving the negro, the Constitution has been trampled under foot, the rights of man have been laughed out of court, and the justice of God has been made a jest and we celebrate.

"Every wire, no longer in the South alone, brings us news of a new hanging or a new burning, some recent outrage against a helpless people, some fresh degradation of an already degraded race. One man sins and a whole nation suffers, and we celebrate.

"Like a dark cloud, pregnant with terror

While remaining a popular poet, Dunbar became well known in his day for writing powerful articles on important social issues. Shown here is an article he wrote on racial injustice that was printed in the New York Times.

self as much a leader in the struggle for civil rights as he was in the arts.

Dunbar had another battle on his hands as well. Coughing virtually all of the time, he tried to make it through another winter at the library while keeping up his schedule of writing and giving public readings. But the chilly wind off the Potomac River proved to be too much for him. His wife continued to press him to quit his job, arguing that with three books in print and a musical play on the road, it was the perfect time to try to survive on a writer's income. Her own book would be coming out before long, and that would bring in some money, too.

Weak and feverish, Dunbar finally agreed that she was right. He handed in his resignation, effective New Year's Day 1899, and then celebrated his decision by inviting a group of friends to his home for a buffet dinner. He did not feel much like partying, though. Despite his wife's assurances, he knew that

Thomas Talley watches as one of his students conducts an experiment in the laboratory of Professor George Washington Carver at the Tuskegee Normal and Industrial Institute. Dunbar visited the celebrated Alabama school in 1899.

making a living as a writer was more than a full-time job; and despite his own assurances to her, he was not sure how long he could continue at even such a reduced pace.

However, other aspects of Dunbar's life were going well. His fame continued to spread throughout the country—so much so that he was becoming embarrassed to hear himself introduced time after time at readings as "the poet laureate of the Negro race." And he undertook a lecture tour that was in many ways more stimulating than his trip to England had been.

In early 1899, the author of *Folks from Dixie* traveled into the Deep South for the first time. One of his destinations was the Tuskegee Normal and Industrial Institute in Tuskegee, Alabama. Founded by Booker T. Washington in 1881, the college had become the leading educational center for blacks in America.

Over the past few years, Dunbar had argued in the press with Washington over the great educator's insistence that blacks should try to improve themselves economically and gain the favor of whites by learning trade skills. What about the arts? the writer had asked. Shouldn't blacks study to be poets, painters, and composers as well?

However, the two men got along like old friends when they met in Tuskegee. Washington listened intently with his students while Dunbar lectured on the uses of literature, advising them not to forget the needs of the heart and spirit in their struggle to gain knowledge. Then the educator asked Dunbar to write a school song, which the poet set to the tune of "Fair Harvard." Washington also pleased the poet by introducing him to Professor George Washington Carver, who was proving through his experiments with the lowly peanut that blacks could contribute to the sciences. Dunbar was excited to learn from Carver that he had been at the Chicago World's Fair. A young painter then, Carver had entered an oil painting in the exhibit for the state of Iowa.

From Tuskegee, Dunbar's lecture tour progressed up the East Coast. No matter where he went, north or south, the weather was cold. After concluding the tour in Boston, he found that it was necessary to get back home in front of his fireplace and nurse his cough.

Lyrics of the Hearthside, Dunbar's fourth volume of poetry, was published in March 1899. The poems in the collection were all new, and they won over the critics to his side once again. Dunbar's readers agreed that these were some of the most powerful poems he had ever written. They were also some of the gloomiest.

From his sickbed, Dunbar had looked into the future to write his own epitaph in "When All Is Done." The poem opens and closes with the following lines:

> When all is done, and my last word is said,
> And ye who loved me murmur, "He is dead,"
> Let no one weep, for fear that I should know,
> And sorrow too that ye should sorrow so.
>
> * * *
>
> When all is done, say not my day is o'er,
> And that thro' night I seek a dimmer shore:
> Say rather that my morn has just begun,—
> I greet the dawn and not a setting sun,
>   When all is done.

But when he was in an even darker mood, the poet could not find any consolation in dying. He wrote in another poem, "Behind the Arras":

> Poor fooled and foolish soul!
>   Know now that death
> Is but a blind, false door that nowhere leads,
> And gives no hope of exit final, free.

The poet's only real comfort in sickness seemed to be his wife. As the first four lines in "Love's Apotheosis," the opening poem in the new book, said:

> Love me. I care not what the circling years
>   To me may do.
> If, but in spite of time and tears,
>   You prove but true.

He dedicated *Lyrics of the Hearthside*, as he had his novel, to "Alice." And in keeping with his new program, he pushed the dialect poems to the back of the book, daring readers to pass over his more serious efforts.

When springtime came, Dunbar still felt poorly. But when he received an invitation to meet with Theodore Roosevelt, the governor of New York, he felt that he could not turn it down. The Old Rough Rider, as Roosevelt was sometimes called, had led a number of black soldiers to a glorious victory at San Juan Hill in 1898 during the Spanish-American War and had recently launched a bid for the presidency. Dunbar, who liked the governor's attacks on corruption in government and business, was anxious to support him.

Roosevelt wanted Dunbar to speak at a conference in Albany, New York. So at the end of April 1899, the ailing poet caught a train north. Yet Dunbar never made it to Albany. While switching trains in New York City, he collapsed on a platform at the station.

The following morning, his wife and mother were horrified to read in the Washington, D.C., newspapers that the great poet Paul Laurence Dunbar had been stricken and was not expected to live. ◕

Among Dunbar's influential supporters at the turn of the century was New York governor Theodore Roosevelt, who succeeded to the presidency in 1901 following the assassination of William McKinley. Roosevelt is shown here in his "Rough Rider" uniform, which he wore while commanding that colorful cavalry regiment during the Spanish-American War.

7

TO SUFFER
AND TO LOVE

THE DIAGNOSIS OF Dunbar's condition after his collapse in May 1899 was pneumonia. But instead of being placed by a doctor in an overcrowded hospital, the poet was advised to stay at a friend's apartment, with a nurse stationed at his side day and night. Both Dunbar's mother and his wife wanted to come to New York City and help look after him, but there was room for only one of them at the apartment. His wife won out and arrived in the city on the following day. She had a little training as a nurse, and she put it to good use in the following weeks.

Dunbar lay in bed for a month, barely able to raise his head. Friends and admirers stopped by every day to leave flowers or food, but his wife would not let them in to see him, fearing that the commotion would sap his strength. Even William Dean Howells climbed up several flights of steps to see how his young friend was doing.

At the end of May, doctors operated on Dunbar, draining fluid from his lungs. After that, he began to feel better. By the middle of June—with his 27th birthday drawing near—he was able to take a few steps without collapsing into a coughing fit.

In turn-of-the-century America, antibiotics had yet to be discovered. The only additional remedies that Dunbar's doctor could prescribe for him were wine and whiskey to help him feel better and six months of rest in the mountains. Accordingly, the

Although Dunbar was continually plagued by poor health following his physical collapse in the spring of 1899, he remained extremely productive. As he wrote in "Melancholia," "Still, oh, still, my brain is whirling!/ Still runs on my stream of thought;/ I am caught/ In the net fate hath set."

85

After surviving a serious bout with pneumonia, Dunbar retreated with his wife, Alice, to the Catskill Mountains in New York for a lengthy period of rest. They were joined there by Dunbar's childhood friend William "Bud" Burns, who had become a prominent doctor.

Dunbars went to the Catskill Mountains, about 60 miles northwest of New York City, at the end of June.

Surrounded by rolling hills and small streams, the Dunbars took in the countryside, spending part of their time fishing and walking around under the clear Catskill skies. Bud Burns heard that his boyhood friend was sick and dropped everything to join the Dunbars in the hills. For a while, it was just like old times. They played checkers, told jokes, and skipped rocks on the pond. Dunbar's health gradually improved.

Soon, Dunbar was able to write to his mother that his weight was back up to 125 pounds—far less than usual, but on the rise. His wife knew he was almost recovered when she woke up one morning to find him scribbling furiously on a notepad. The poet was back at work again.

Despite Dunbar's show of improved health, Burns advised him not to return to Washington, D.C. Another winter there, the doctor warned, and Dunbar would be right back in bed again. It would be better for him to head west, to a place where the air was always warm and dry.

Dunbar's eyes lit up at Burns's suggestion. He knew just where to go: Denver, Colorado—"the mile-high city"—where the cowboys who filled so many of his childhood short stories still rode along the trails.

When the Dunbars stepped off their train in Denver on September 12, they beheld a sight like none they had ever seen: the snowcapped Rocky Mountains, ranging off into the distance as far as the eye could see. They saw cowboys, too—the real thing, with chaps and boots and the smell of old sweat. It was strange for Dunbar to see these boyhood heroes walking up the street, politely making their way around the wheelchairs and strollers of people who, like himself, had come to Denver for their health.

The Dunbars soon found a pleasant house outside of town and bought a horse and buggy in which to get around. Then the ailing poet set to work on—

what else?—a Western novel. He called it *The Love of Landry*.

In the book, a sickly young woman from the East comes to Denver for a cure and finds not only improved health but romance with a cowboy as well. It was not much of a tale by Dunbar's standards—just a way for him to get back into the habit of writing. Yet even in this little novel he was able to portray chillingly what it felt like to have come so far on the slim hope of better health. In *The Love of Landry*, he wrote:

> With all the faith one may have in one's self, with all the strong hopefulness of youth, it is yet a terrible thing to be forced away from home, from all one loves, to an unknown, uncared-for country, there to fight, hand to hand with death, an uncertain fight. There is none of the rush and clamour of battle that keeps up the soldier's courage. There is no clang of the instruments of war. The panting warrior hears no loud huzzas, and yet the deadly combat goes on; in the still night, when all the world's asleep, in the grey day, in the pale morning, it goes on, and no one knows it save himself and death.

When the Dunbars arrived by train in Denver, Colorado, in September 1899, they were greeted by a sight much like the one shown here, with the Rocky Mountains towering in the background of the western city.

The 20th century dawned with Dunbar feeling that he had won, if not the war, then at least the battle for his health. He and his wife moved back to Washington, D.C., for the summer of 1900, and when he spoke to his editor at Dodd, Mead & Company, he was pleased to learn that *Lyrics of Lowly Life* and an illustrated book of poems entitled *Poems of Cabin and Field* were still selling in the thousands each year. Dunbar now rivaled his old hero James Whitcomb Riley as one of the most popular poets in the country.

Unfortunately for Dunbar, when he went to New York City to collect his money, his luck turned sour again. On August 15, shortly after he arrived a race riot broke out in midtown, with gangs of whites roaming the streets, beating every black they could find. Dunbar slipped away only after he had been robbed of six months' worth of royalties.

When Dunbar returned to the nation's capital, he was told by a doctor that he was still too sick to travel very much. Yet with his money gone there was little else for him to do but to hit the road once again on a lecture tour. This time he journeyed to the familiar haunts of the Midwest, where he had read hundreds of times before.

Often on the tour it seemed to Dunbar that he should not have gone. On some mornings, he woke up with stained sheets, having spit up blood during the night. He could barely catch his breath after walking up a flight of steps. It was becoming increasingly obvious that he had tuberculosis, which was then called consumption.

The only treatment then known for tuberculosis was bed rest, sometimes for years—and even that did not always save the patient. Dunbar, who had always worked harder and faster than most other men, could not understand why, after a year of rest and relaxation, he could not throw himself back into the swing of things. After all, he was only 28 years old, in the prime of his life. However, his lungs were those of a sick old man.

In October, Dunbar was late for a reading at a church in Evanston, Illinois. When he finally arrived, a doctor and a nurse were by his side. The audience, which remembered his booming voice and rollicking humor, had waited quietly for his arrival. But when Dunbar began to read, his booming voice was no longer present. He mumbled, stumbled over his lines, and coughed.

Everyone in the audience waited for Dunbar to regain his composure. They were afraid to think about what might be wrong with him. Then one person after another whispered, "He's drunk." This was a particularly terrible accusation to have to face in Evanston, which served as a home base for the temperance movement, a national campaign aimed at stamping out liquor. People stood up and stormed out of the church, so outraged at the poet that they could not wait to tell their friends.

The story of Dunbar's reading showed up in the local paper on the following day, prompting him to write an apology to the editor. He explained his poor performance by saying that he was not in good health and admitted that he had taken a few drinks to ease his pain. In fact, he was often drinking a bit more than that.

The incident proved to be a turning point in Dunbar's career, for he realized at last that he could no longer do the work of several men. He wrote to a friend, "I have cancelled all my engagements and given up reading entirely. They are trying to force me back to Denver, but I am ill and discouraged, and do not much care what happens."

Although Dunbar could not tour any more, he could still write. From the middle of September to the end of November, he produced several short stories and poems, as well as a novel, *The Fanatics*. After that output, he proudly told a friend, "I am going to

According to Current Literature, *a literary magazine that frequently featured poems written by Dunbar, his verses "are graceful, lyrical and imaginative and richly deserve the popularity which they have received."*

give myself a little vacation for a while right here at home. I shall smoke and read and play cards and make the night (and day as well) hideous with my violin. How long this will last it is hard to tell, for it takes only a short time for the bee of unrest to sting me into activity."

As Dunbar had suggested to his friend, the sting came quickly. He sent off *The Fanatics* to Dodd, Mead & Company, then started in right after Christmas on a new novel, which he finished in four weeks—just in time to accept what he considered to be one of the great honors of his career. He had been asked to ride in the inaugural parade of President William McKinley through the streets of Washington, D.C., on March 4, 1901. Even though Dunbar had never ridden a horse before, he took part in the parade. Both his wife and his mother said he looked as dignified as a soldier up in the saddle (for the parade, he was given the honorary rank of colonel).

In March 1901, James Weldon Johnson invited Dunbar to visit him in Jacksonville, Florida, prom-

William McKinley gives his first inaugural address after being elected to the presidency in 1896. Dunbar was invited to participate in McKinley's inaugural parade after the president was reelected in 1900.

ising his fellow writer clear skies and sunshine. Despite the warm weather, Dunbar still could not shake his cough. His doctors were unable to help him, and so he turned to quack remedies. Johnson did not know whether to be amused or appalled at the raw onion and mug of beer that his friend consumed before going to bed every night.

Dunbar gave two readings while in Jacksonville. Because his father had fought there during the Civil War, he made a point of reciting poems that he had written about soldiers. To accompany Dunbar's readings, Johnson had a local band strike up a marching beat. The bass drums perfectly matched the martial rhythms of Dunbar's poems. "His voice was a perfect musical instrument," Johnson said, "and he knew how to use it with extreme effect."

Johnson, who labored over his own poems for weeks at a time, could not get over the rapid way in which Dunbar worked. The aspiring poet said of his guest, "During his visit he wrote a half dozen or so poems. As quickly as he finished them he sent them off; two of them, I remember, to the Saturday Evening Post; and I was amazed at seeing how promptly he received checks in return. Whatever he wrote was in demand."

Even though most of his work had been well received, Dunbar told Johnson that a poet's life was not as easy as it looked. He pointed out how hard it had been for him to find an audience for his serious work. "I didn't start with dialect," he said, "but dialect is what people want. They won't let me do anything else, no matter how much I try. I've got to write dialect if I want them to listen."

On this point, Johnson thought Dunbar was being too hard on himself. After all, the 29-year-old poet had published a lot of verse that was not in dialect. Besides, the poems in dialect were some of Johnson's favorite pieces as well. He had already begun to write dialect poems to launch his own career. Johnson's

Dunbar rode in President William McKinley's inaugural parade in March 1901. The poet is shown here on his horse, Old Sukey.

poems would ultimately depart from Dunbar's rhythmic voicings and employ free verse, a form of poetry that does not contain a regular meter.

Encouraged and rested after six weeks at Johnson's house in Florida, Dunbar took his time getting back to Washington, D.C. Along the way, he stopped off at Tuskegee Institute and other colleges—including Atlanta University in Atlanta, Georgia, where he was awarded an honorary M.A. degree. He was happy to discover at these schools that some students were earning money for their tuition by reading his poems aloud. He stopped at home just long enough to collect his wife and a few belongings, and then continued his working vacation at a cabin on Chesapeake Bay.

Soon, the Dunbars were back in the nation's capital. Both of them had been bitten by disease-ridden mosquitoes and had come down with malaria. They convalesced at home for most of the summer, recovering just in time to make another trip—this time to Kentucky, where the poet's cousin Ella Burton was starring in the title role of *Clorindy*.

By then, Dunbar's latest novel had turned up in the nation's bookstores. Unlike his previous novel, *The Fanatics* was not a simple cowboy-and-Indian tale. Rather, it was a serious effort to show how blacks and whites had coped with emancipation in the years after the Civil War.

In writing *The Fanatics*, Dunbar had particularly wanted to explore the difficult position that people in the North were in at a time when thousands of freed slaves—Dunbar's mother among them—had poured in to find a better way of life. It was an opportunity to delve into the many subtle aspects of the race problem, such as the way that blacks who had already been in the North for a while actually joined forces with whites for a time to conspire against other blacks. "All party lines fell away," he wrote, "and all the people are united in one cause—resistance to the invasion of the black hordes."

Though *The Fanatics* looked unflinchingly at how difficult it was for blacks to attain full acceptance as citizens, the novel also depicted how disheartening it was for former slaves to be free at last—only to run into a stone wall again. "Was this the freedom for which they had toiled?" the author asked. As the 20th century began, blacks all over America were asking themselves that very question.

Dunbar's next novel, *The Sport of the Gods*, looked even more closely at the struggle of his people. Although he finished it in just one month, it was nevertheless the most accomplished work of fiction he would ever write. As in *The Fanatics*, he painstakingly revealed the complexities of dealings between whites and blacks. However, in this new novel he moved the action to the present and focused on a southern black family's efforts to find a niche for itself in the modern world.

By the time that *The Sport of the Gods* was published in 1902, a few American writers had already begun to speak plainly in their work about life as it was actually lived. Yet most authors made their living by telling upbeat tales with happy endings. Dunbar was well known for his sentimental stories of old plantation life, so his readers must have been shocked to open his latest book and find it filled instead with stark realism.

The narrative begins in a small southern town, where the novel's main character goes to jail for a crime that he did not commit. When blacks and whites alike turn away from his family, the family moves to New York City for a new start. But life in the big city proves to be difficult for them, and they are unable to cope. One son becomes a drunk and a murderer, a daughter ends up as a second-rate show girl, and the mother marries a low-rent gambler who treats her badly.

Dunbar brings the family together again in the end. Any other conclusion would have been too much

Poet Claude McKay was one of the leading figures in the Harlem Renaissance, the ground-breaking black cultural movement that took place in the 1920s. By encouraging white America to look at blacks as fellow citizens, Dunbar helped pave the way for the achievements of black writers.

for his readers to handle. But this time, he had stepped out on a limb to tell a few harsh truths about how hard it could be for blacks to succeed in America.

It was not until 20 years after *The Sport of the Gods* was published that other black writers would follow in Dunbar's footsteps and cause a sensation with their realistic look at black life, especially in the New York City district of Harlem. Among the writers who led the black artistic and intellectual movement in the 1920s that came to be known as the Harlem Renaissance were the poets Langston Hughes and Claude McKay. "We younger Negro artists who create now intend to express our individual dark-skinned selves without fear or shame," Hughes declared in 1926. But in the early 1900s, Dunbar was virtually on his own, daring his readers to face the hard struggle of one black family in America.

On New Year's Day in 1902, Dunbar felt strong enough to accept an invitation to the White House. Theodore Roosevelt, the newly appointed president of the United States, had invited celebrities from all walks of life to attend a formal reception. Shortly after Dunbar arrived at the White House, he stood on a receiving line to greet the president, who proceeded to embarrass the poet by pulling him out of the line to praise him loudly in front of the other guests.

Despite this happy occasion, the early part of 1902 marked a difficult time for Dunbar and his wife. His health required constant attention. People were always knocking on their door to propose some new venture or just to shake his hand. Consequently, Alice rarely had time for her own writing. Sometimes, they fought, and as his father had done, Dunbar often found himself storming out of the house in a rage. On these occasions, his behavior may have been affected by a growing drinking problem.

One night, they began to argue in front of Alice's parents, who were visiting for a few days. In the heat

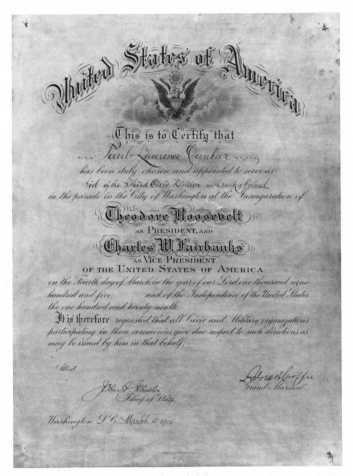

In 1902, Dunbar attended a reception given by President Theodore Roosevelt at the White House. The certificate shown here acknowledges the poet's participation at Roosevelt's second inauguration, held three years later.

of the battle, Alice ordered her husband out of the house. Dunbar stomped off, not even bothering to grab his hat.

If this fight had taken place at some other time, the poet might have walked around a bit along the icy streets, allowing his anger to cool. Then he would have returned to the house and patched things up with his wife. That was what had always happened before. But this time, Dunbar did something that he would later regret. Instead of going home, he went straight to the railway station, bought a one-way ticket, and caught a train to New York City. There was no way he could have guessed it then, but he would never see Alice again.

8

I GREET THE DAWN

EARLY IN FEBRUARY 1902, Dunbar wrote to his mother in Dayton about his "trouble" with Alice. "She was in the wrong," he said, "but she won't write to me, won't send me my mail or any of my clothes. . . . I am nearly crazy." By the time their fourth wedding anniversary arrived one month later, Alice still had not written to him.

Dunbar soon heard that his wife had begun to reorganize her life without him, signing on as a schoolteacher in Washington, D.C. He was crushed by the news. Often pacing the rainy streets of New York City for hours, he began to write mournful poems. At last, he wore himself down to such a point that a doctor ordered him into the Toledo State Hospital in Ohio. Dunbar remained there until he had recuperated.

Will Marion Cook tried to keep his old friend's mind off his marital troubles by getting him involved in another musical production. Together, they wrote a play called *In Dahomey*. After opening in New York City, the production toured England and even entertained British royalty at Buckingham Palace.

Unimpressed with the play's success, a heartsick Dunbar traveled to Chicago to visit his two brothers. They were shocked to see him so thin and shocked again to hear him say that he could no longer write. He said at the time, "Something within me seems to be dead. There is not spirit or energy left in me."

As Dunbar's physical and mental health grew increasingly poorer in 1902, a physician ordered him to convalesce in the Toledo State Hospital. He is shown here fishing on the hospital's grounds.

97

Dunbar talked about going into some sort of business with his brother Rob, but no one took him seriously. All his brothers could do was stand by and catch him when he at last suffered a nervous breakdown and developed pneumonia. Summoned from Dayton, his mother nursed him night and day. The poet gradually recovered, surprising her one day by asking if he could return with her to Dayton.

On the way home from Chicago, Dunbar stopped at Toledo to visit Dr. Tobey, who, like the poet's family, must have been dismayed by Dunbar's haggard appearance. After all the favors that the doctor had granted to him over the years, Dunbar still had one more to ask. He pleaded with the doctor to write to Alice on his behalf. Dr. Tobey did so, but apparently to no effect.

Back in Dayton, Dunbar suffered another collapse and was in bed more often than not. But when he heard that the Wright brothers were back in town, he gathered his strength and went to see them. The

Bert Williams (left) and George Walker (right), one of the nation's most popular black minstrel teams, are shown in 1903 in the New York City production of In Dahomey, *a musical comedy written by Dunbar and composer Will Marion Cook.*

Wrights had just returned from Kitty Hawk, North Carolina, where Orville had stretched out on his stomach between the wings of a spindly looking gliding contraption that had flown with the wind across Kitty Hawk's barren sand dunes. Excited by their accomplishment, they were making plans to add an engine and propeller to the glider so it could fly on its own power.

The Wrights were happy to see their old friend, who knew so much of the fame that they would taste in the years ahead. On December 13, 1903, Orville would make the first powered flight in history. However, even the Wright brothers could not cheer up Dunbar.

Although ill and depressed, Dunbar somehow found the resolve to write more poems and to contribute editorials to some of the nation's major newspapers. These were some of his angriest writings, pointing out the hypocrisy of a nation that touted freedom but withheld the right to vote and the right to equal employment from many of its citizens. His anger came to a head in the article he published in the *Chicago Tribune* on the Fourth of July, 1903:

On December 17, 1903, Dunbar's boyhood friends Orville and Wilbur Wright made aviation history by launching the world's first man-carrying powered flight at Kitty Hawk, North Carolina. Orville piloted the first flight, which lasted for 12 seconds and covered about 120 feet.

Dunbar and a friend in front of his home during his waning years in Dayton.

Every wire—no longer from the South alone—brings us news of a new hanging or a new burning, some recent outrage against a helpless people. . . . Like a dark cloud pregnant with terror and destruction disfranchisement has spread its wings over our brethren of the South. Like the same dark cloud industrial prejudice glooms above us in the North. . . . And yet we celebrate.

During that same month, *Lyrics of Love and Laughter*, Dunbar's new collection of poems, came out. Despite the book's cheerful title, many of its poems revealed the poet's increasing despair over his circumstances. One poem, entitled "The Debt," powerfully expressed his sadness over the breakup with his wife:

> This is the debt I pay
> Just for one riotous day,
> Years of regret and grief,
> Sorrow without relief.
>
> Pay it I will to the end—
> Until the grave, my friend,
> Gives me a true release—
> Gives me the clasp of peace.

Slight was the thing I bought,
Small was the debt I thought,
Poor was the loan at best—
God! but the interest!

This poem, like others in *Lyrics of Love and Laughter*, reveals a more economical and lighter touch than Dunbar's earlier poems. Even while on a sickbed, he had continued to hone his craft.

In publishing *Lyrics of Love and Laughter*, Dunbar's editor had won in his effort to highlight the poet's dialect pieces. Whereas these poems had been placed toward the back in his last several volumes, the very first poem in this collection was in dialect, and similar pieces were scattered throughout the book. Dunbar did not have the strength to argue over this arrangement. But he did insert a subtle protest into the collection. Entitled "The Poet," the poem movingly expressed his disappointment over failing to win approval for any pieces but his dialect poems:

He sang of life, serenely sweet,
    With, now and then, a deeper note.
    From some high peak, nigh yet remote,
He voiced the world's absorbing beat.

He sang of love when earth was young,
    And Love, itself, was in his lays.
    But ah, the world, it turned to praise
A jingle in a broken tongue.

Eventually, Dunbar managed to find comfort in his boyhood haunts around Dayton. The house that he had bought for his mother while he was an elevator operator began to seem run-down, so he moved her to a newer one, near the Wright brothers' house. His longtime friend Bud Burns stopped by to visit and check on his health almost every evening. They played checkers and told each other jokes. Dunbar also found time to teach reading to a few adults in the neighborhood who had never before had the chance to learn.

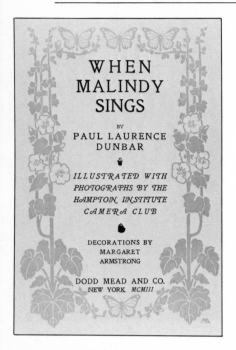

WHEN
MALINDY
SINGS

BY
PAUL LAURENCE
DUNBAR

ILLUSTRATED WITH
PHOTOGRAPHS BY THE
HAMPTON INSTITUTE
CAMERA CLUB

DECORATIONS BY
MARGARET
ARMSTRONG

DODD MEAD AND CO.
NEW YORK MCMIII

Published in 1903, When Mal-indy Sings *was one of several books by Dunbar to be ornately designed and illustrated.*

In December 1903, Dunbar stopped by the Wright brothers' house, only to learn that they were back in Kitty Hawk, trying to fly their propeller-driven airplane. He read the telegram they had just sent home— a document that later served as proof to the world that his friends had launched the era of aviation:

FOUR FLIGHTS THURSDAY MORNING. ALL AGAINST 21 MILE WIND. STARTED FROM LEVEL WITH ENGINE POWER ALONE. AVERAGE SPEED THROUGH AIR 31 MILES. LONGEST 852 FEET 59 SECONDS. INFORM PRESS. HOME CHRIST-MAS.

Flushed with their success, the Wrights immediately built a hangar outside of Dayton where they continued to conduct their experiments. After years of trial and error, they had begun to make their mark on the world. Dunbar saw them on only a few occasions after their historic flight.

In late 1903, Dunbar issued a new book of short stories, *In Old Plantation Days.* Sales of the book were brisk at Christmas time. Another volume of short stories, *The Heart of Happy Hollow,* was published in the spring of 1904 but sold more slowly.

Dunbar's readers might have expected the second book of short stories to be filled with nostalgic and sentimental tales like the first, but he again took the opportunity to experiment with realism in several of the stories in the new collection. In the preface to *The Heart of Happy Hollow,* he advised the reader that he had written about working-class blacks in "the cities or villages, north or south, wherever the hod carrier [laborer], the porter and the waiter are the society men of the town." One story depicted a lynching; another told about the life of an unsung hero whom the poet knew well: a washerwoman like his mother.

Any writer would have been proud of completing so much work in such a short period of time. But when James Weldon Johnson came to visit Dunbar, he heard the noted poet complain, "I've kept on doing the same things. I've never gotten to do the things I really wanted to do most. I haven't grown. I'm writing the same things I wrote 10 years ago and writing them no better."

Dunbar had dreamed of drafting a history of black Americans. He envisioned the work as expanding into several volumes as the writing progressed. However, the poet had begun to doubt that he would ever begin the project.

Johnson did all that he could to cheer up his ailing friend, reminding him of the broad range of his accomplishments in poetry, fiction, social criticism, and the theater. He must have struck a sympathetic note at some point because when Dunbar's illustrated book of poems Li'l' Gal came out in October 1904, the 32-year-old poet sent Dr. Tobey a copy with this proud inscription: "This is my seventeenth book: that's what you get for encouraging youthful ambition—and you did, you can't deny it."

By Christmas, Dunbar had written enough poems for a new volume of original verse. Entitled Lyrics of Sunshine and Shadow, it was the last collection that he ever produced. Two poems in the collection can be read as companion pieces that sum up Dunbar's view of his life and art. The first poem, "Compensation," reads:

Verses in Dunbar's 17th book, Li'l' Gal, continued to reflect his sorrow over the breakup of his marriage. Among the poetry that reflected this lovelorn attitude was the title poem, written in dialect and containing the line, "I's so'y I cain't 'spress it w'en I knows I loves you true."

> Because I had loved so deeply,
>   Because I had loved so long,
> God in His great compassion
>   Gave me the gift of song.
>
> Because I have loved so vainly,
>   And sung with such faltering breath,
> The Master in infinite mercy
>   Offers the boon of Death.

The second poem, "Encouraged," is a parting "thank you" to all the people who had helped him during his career:

A photograph of Matilda Dunbar taken after her son's death. Her faith and devotion were a constant source of inspiration to Dunbar, who wrote in a poem entitled "When All Is Done," "Say rather that my morn has just begun, —/ I greet the dawn and not a setting sun, / When all is done."

Because you love me I have much achieved,
    Had you despised me then I must have failed,
But since I knew you trusted and believed,
    I could not disappoint you and so prevailed.

Meanwhile, Dunbar pleaded with his wife in letter after letter to come see him again. Not only did she fail to visit him, but she never wrote back.

Dunbar had believed for some time that his days were numbered, and in November 1905, he suffered a major blow: Bud Burns died suddenly. Dunbar's mother begged her son not to attend Burns's funeral and risk the damp wind at the cemetery, but he would not listen to her. He stood bareheaded during the funeral services while his friend's body was lowered into the ground. Devastated by Burns's death, Dunbar wrote at Christmas, "Like the fields I am lying fallow. And it will take a long time to make anything worth coming out in blossom."

It was a bitter winter in Dayton. The new year came around blowing snow and ice. Dunbar's mother made a bed for her son by the fire in the living room, where he could rest and keep warm. But on February 9, 1906, his ravaged lungs gave out at last. Paul Laurence Dunbar died in his mother's arms at the age of 33.

The poet from Dayton, Ohio, had traveled all over the United States and Europe, only to come full circle and be buried in his hometown. Dr. Tobey spoke at Dunbar's funeral. But it was another old friend, Brand Whitlock, who wrote what may have been the poet's finest obituary. In a letter to Dunbar's mother, he said, "You have lost a son, I have lost a friend, but America has lost more than all else and that is a poet."

Dunbar's wife, Alice, eventually remarried. Yet Dunbar's writings continued to engross her. She quietly began to promote his work in articles and essays that she contributed to the Associated Negro Press, a black news service. She also edited two books that included pieces by him, *Masterpieces of Negro Eloquence* and *The Dunbar Speaker*.

Until her death at the age of 95, Matilda Dunbar continued to live in the house that her son had shared with her. Eventually, the house at 219 North Summit Street became a national shrine in his honor, and it can still be visited in Dayton today. Schools, banks, and hospitals all over the country have been named in honor of the poet.

Dunbar's greatest legacy, however, is his work. No one can say how many readers have been inspired by his ringing, soul-searching lines. To the younger writers of his age, it is plain that he was a hero. James Weldon Johnson, Langston Hughes, and Claude McKay have written of their debt to him, and scholars agree that he set the stage for the renaissance in black art that took place in the 1920s.

Had Dunbar lived to an old age, he would undoubtedly have achieved even more. But as it stands, his work is a vital and varied chronicle of a young man who believed in the power of love, compassion, and imagination. From the most joyful of moments to the most despairing, he accepted the challenge of finding words to express all that he knew and felt. With the same courage that he summoned up to fight a deadly disease, he battled racism and misunderstanding between the races.

A child of former slaves, Paul Laurence Dunbar dared to believe that the United States might someday be a place where everyone of every race could live happily and well. His most cheerful lines soar with that hope; his more somber lines show that he knew the road would be long. It is a testament to his powers as a poet that so many have taken him at his word and have chosen to follow in his footsteps. ❧

Dunbar's home on North Summit Street in Dayton is now open to the public as a museum.

APPENDIX

BOOKS BY
PAUL LAURENCE DUNBAR

Many of the following titles, originally published around the turn of the century, are now available in reprint editions.

POETRY
1892	*Oak and Ivy*
1896	*Majors and Minors*
1896	*Lyrics of Lowly Life*
1899	*Lyrics of the Hearthside*
1899	*Poems of Cabin and Field*
1901	*Candle Lightin' Time*
1903	*Lyrics of Love and Laughter*
1903	*When Malindy Sings*
1903	*Lyrics of Sunshine and Shadow*
1904	*L'il' Gal*
1905	*Howdy, Honey, Howdy*
1913	*Complete Poems*

SHORT STORIES
1898	*Folks from Dixie*
1900	*The Strength of Gideon and Other Stories*
1903	*In Old Plantation Days*
1904	*The Heart of Happy Hollow*

NOVELS
1898	*The Uncalled*
1900	*The Love of Landry*
1901	*The Fanatics*
1902	*The Sport of the Gods*

CHRONOLOGY

June 27, 1872	Born Paul Laurence Dunbar in Dayton, Ohio
1888	First poem, "Our Martyred Soldiers," is published
1891	Dunbar graduates from Central High School in Dayton
1892	First book, *Oak and Ivy*, is published
1893	Dunbar attends the World's Columbian Exposition in Chicago, Illinois; works with Frederick Douglass
1896	*Majors and Minors* and *Lyrics of Lowly Life* are published; receives worldwide acclaim
1897	Dunbar tours England; collaborates with Samuel Coleridge-Taylor on musical works; accepts position as assistant librarian at the Library of Congress
1898	Marries Alice Ruth Moore; *Folks from Dixie* and *The Uncalled* are published; collaborates with Will Marion Cook on *Clorindy*
1899	*Lyrics of the Hearthside* is published; Dunbar collapses from pneumonia; convalesces in Denver, Colorado
1900	*Love of Landry* and *Poems of Cabin and Field* are published
1901	*The Fanatics* is published
1902	*The Sport of the Gods* is published; collaborates with Cook on *In Dahomey*; separates permanently from wife
1903	Dunbar resettles in Dayton; *Lyrics of Love and Laughter, In Old Plantation Days*, and *When Malindy Sings* are published
1904	*The Heart of Happy Hollow* and *Li'l' Gal* are published
1905	*Lyrics of Sunshine and Shadow* is published
Feb. 9, 1906	Dunbar dies of tuberculosis in Dayton, Ohio

FURTHER READING

Brawley, Benjamin. *Paul Laurence Dunbar: A Poet of His People*. Chapel Hill: University of North Carolina Press, 1936.

Cunningham, Virginia. *Paul Laurence Dunbar and His Song*. New York: Biblio & Tannen, 1969.

Gayle, Addison, Jr. *Oak and Ivy: A Biography of Paul Laurence Dunbar*. Garden City, NY: Doubleday, 1971.

Hughes, Langston. "Paul Laurence Dunbar, the Robert Burns of Negro Poetry." In *Famous American Negroes*. New York: Dodd, Mead, 1975.

Lawson, Victor. *A Singer in the Dawn: Reinterpretations of Paul Laurence Dunbar*. New York: Dodd, Mead, 1975.

McKissack, Pat. *Paul Laurence Dunbar: A Poet to Remember*. Chicago: Children's Press, 1984.

Martin, Jay, and Gossie H. Hudson, eds. *The Paul Laurence Dunbar Reader*. New York: Dodd, Mead, 1975.

Revell, Peter. *Paul Laurence Dunbar*. Boston: Twayne Publishers, 1979.

Schultz, Pearle H. *Paul Laurence Dunbar: Black Poet Laureate*. Champaign, IL: Garrad Publishing Company, 1974.

Wiggins, Lida Keck, ed. *The Life and Works of Paul Laurence Dunbar*. Napierville, IL: J. L. Nichols, 1907.

INDEX

110

PICTURE CREDITS

TONY GENTRY holds an honors degree in history and literature from Harvard College. Formerly an award-winning news and feature editor at WWL Newsradio in New Orleans, he now lives and works in New York City. His poetry and short stories have been published in several literary magazines and journals, including *Downtown* and *Turnstile*. He has recently completed his first novel, *Louisiana Live Oak*.

NATHAN IRVIN HUGGINS is W.E.B. Du Bois Professor of History and Director of the W.E.B. Du Bois Institute for Afro-American Research at Harvard University. He previously taught at Columbia University. Professor Huggins is the author of numerous books, including *Black Odyssey: The Afro-American Ordeal in Slavery*, *The Harlem Renaissance*, and *Slave and Citizen: The Life of Frederick Douglass*.